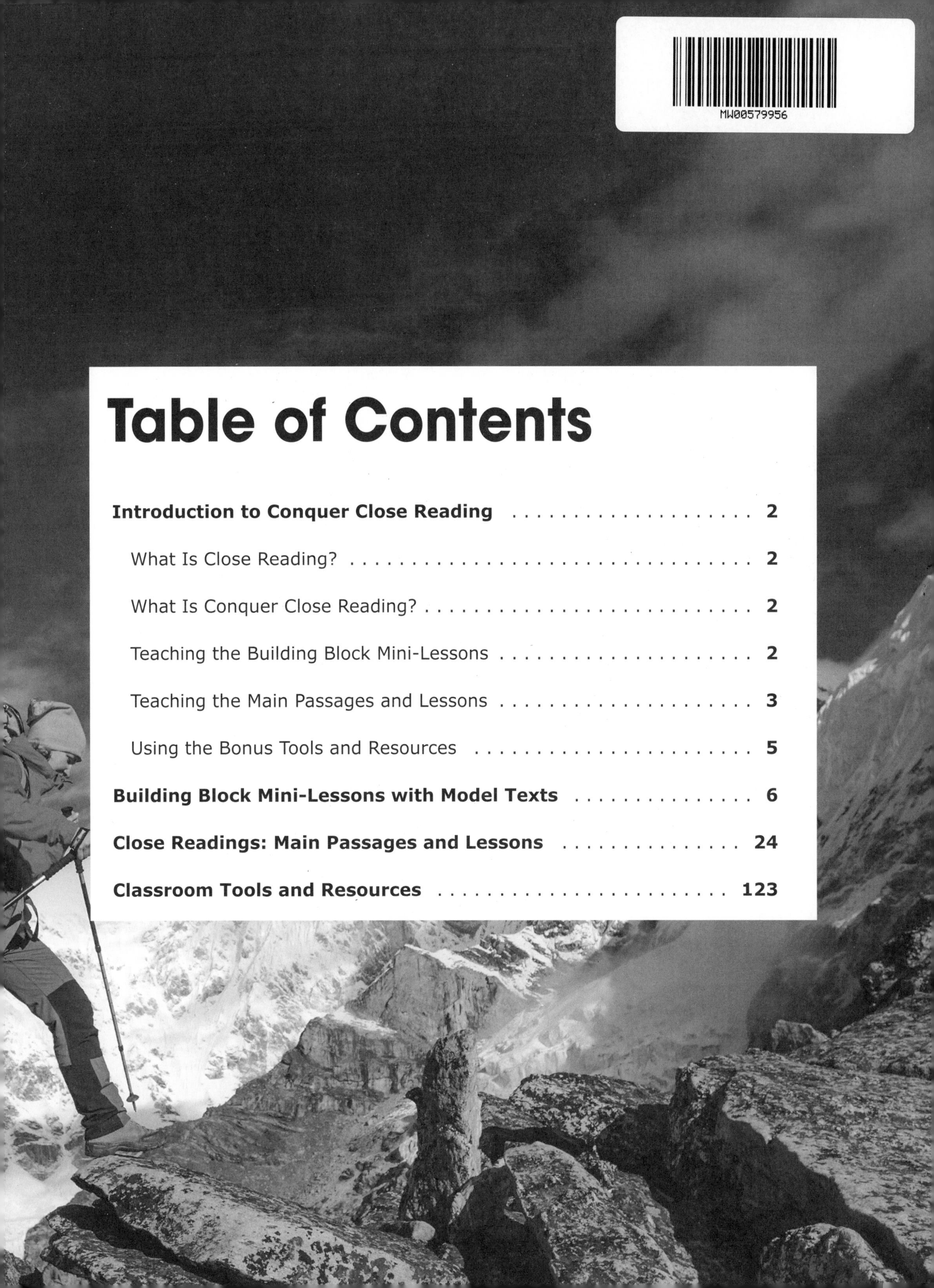

Table of Contents

Introduction

What Is Close Reading?

Rigorous standards for English Language Arts place new demands on students and teachers. Students are expected to read and comprehend complex literary and informational texts independently and proficiently. One way to achieve this level of text comprehension is through close reading. Close reading features repeated readings of a text with each reading focused on a specific aspect of the text, for instance, vocabulary or text structure. Through the close reading process, students build up their understanding gradually, so by the end they have a thorough understanding of what they read.

What Is Conquer Close Reading?

Conquer Close Reading is a series of reproducible books for Grades 2–6 that helps students learn to engage in a close reading of a text so that over time they can successfully understand, analyze, and evaluate the ideas in complex texts independently. Students first build close reading skills and then practice and apply them so they develop and hone the skills and abilities necessary to comprehend the increasingly complex texts they will encounter.

In Conquer Close Reading, students learn to unlock the meaning of text by:

- Reading and annotating passages in a variety of genres
- Engaging in close readings and collaborative conversations about the texts
- Examining the vocabulary authors use
- Analyzing text structure of both literary and informational texts
- Evaluating the "big ideas" proposed in texts
- Writing about what they've read and discussed using text evidence

Teaching the Building Block Mini-Lessons

Each grade of Conquer Close Reading begins with two sample texts—one literary and one informational—and a series of twelve mini-lessons. The mini-lessons use the passages to build the skills students need to read closely for deep meaning.

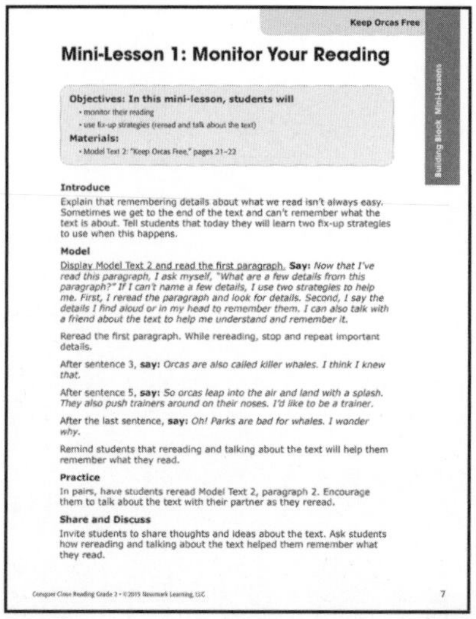
Keep Orcas Free

Building Block Mini-Lessons

Mini-Lesson 1: Monitor Your Reading

Objectives: In this mini-lesson, students will
- monitor their reading
- use fix-up strategies (reread and talk about the text)

Materials:
- Model Text 2: "Keep Orcas Free," pages 21–22

Introduce

Explain that remembering details about what we read isn't always easy. Sometimes we get to the end of the text and can't remember what the text is about. Tell students that today they will learn two fix-up strategies to use when this happens.

Model

Display Model Text 2 and read the first paragraph. **Say:** *Now that I've read this paragraph, I ask myself, "What are a few details from this paragraph?" If I can't name a few details, I use two strategies to help me. First, I reread the paragraph and look for details. Second, I say the details I find aloud or in my head to remember them. I can also talk with a friend about the text to help me understand and remember it.*

Reread the first paragraph. While rereading, stop and repeat important details.

After sentence 3, **say:** *Orcas are also called killer whales. I think I knew that.*

After sentence 5, **say:** *So orcas leap into the air and land with a splash. They also push trainers around on their noses. I'd like to be a trainer.*

After the last sentence, **say:** *Oh! Parks are bad for whales. I wonder why.*

Remind students that rereading and talking about the text will help them remember what they read.

Practice

In pairs, have students reread Model Text 2, paragraph 2. Encourage them to talk about the text with their partner as they reread.

Share and Discuss

Invite students to share thoughts and ideas about the text. Ask students how rereading and talking about the text helped them remember what they read.

Conquer Close Reading Grade 2 • ©2015 Newmark Learning, LLC 7

Teaching the Main Passages and Lessons

Each of the fourteen main lessons in Conquer Close Reading features a passage—either literary or informational—that students read and reread to practice and apply the close reading skills they've acquired during instruction of the mini-lessons.

As you start instruction using Conquer Close Reading, keep in mind that students need the opportunity to grapple with the ideas they find in text. They should read the passages independently the first time. Avoid front-loading information or pre-teaching vocabulary. This will allow students to first notice what is confusing so they develop a habit they can use when they read on their own.

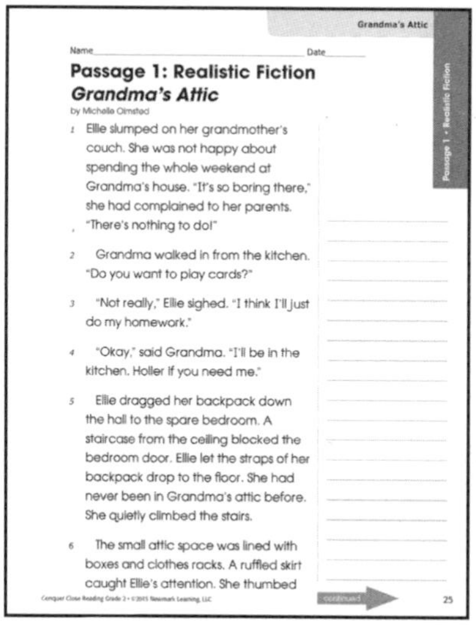

Grandma's Attic

Name________________ Date________

Passage 1: Realistic Fiction

Grandma's Attic

by Michelle Olmsted

1 Ellie slumped on her grandmother's couch. She was not happy about spending the whole weekend at Grandma's house. "It's so boring there," she had complained to her parents. "There's nothing to do!"

2 Grandma walked in from the kitchen. "Do you want to play cards?"

3 "Not really," Ellie sighed. "I think I'll just do my homework."

4 "Okay," said Grandma. "I'll be in the kitchen. Holler if you need me."

5 Ellie dragged her backpack down the hall to the spare bedroom. A staircase from the ceiling blocked the bedroom door. Ellie let the straps of her backpack drop to the floor. She had never been in Grandma's attic before. She quietly climbed the stairs.

6 The small attic space was lined with boxes and clothes racks. A ruffled skirt caught Ellie's attention. She thumbed

Passage 1 • Realistic Fiction

Conquer Close Reading Grade 2 • ©2015 Newmark Learning, LLC 25

Step 1

The first reading focuses on gaining a general understanding of the text. The students summarize what they read by identifying what the text is mostly about. They also identify key details necessary for understanding. The first reading culminates in a collaborative conversation, giving students an opportunity to build speaking and listening skills, broaden their point of view, and build vocabulary as they compare their impressions of the text and prepare to delve into it in greater detail.

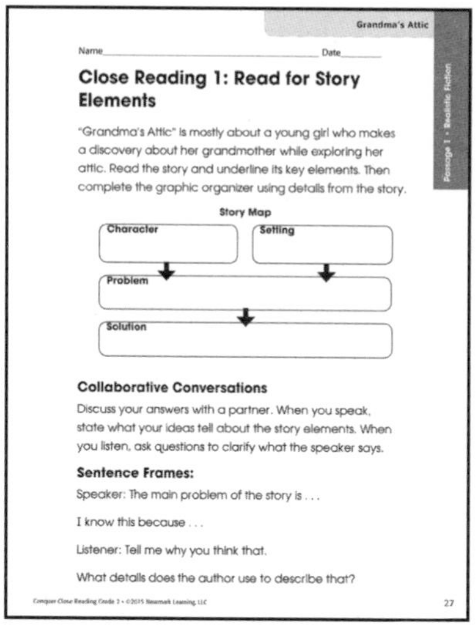

Grandma's Attic

Name________________ Date________

Close Reading 1: Read for Story Elements

"Grandma's Attic" is mostly about a young girl who makes a discovery about her grandmother while exploring her attic. Read the story and underline its key elements. Then complete the graphic organizer using details from the story.

Collaborative Conversations

Discuss your answers with a partner. When you speak, state what your ideas tell about the story elements. When you listen, ask questions to clarify what the speaker says.

Sentence Frames:

Speaker: The main problem of the story is . . .

I know this because . . .

Listener: Tell me why you think that.

What details does the author use to describe that?

Passage 1 • Realistic Fiction

Conquer Close Reading Grade 2 • ©2015 Newmark Learning, LLC 27

Step 2

The second reading starts the building of a deeper understanding of the text. This reading focuses on four to six vocabulary words: Tier 2 words, challenging words, or examples of figurative language. Students use context to determine word meaning, the connotation in the text, and why the author chose the word.

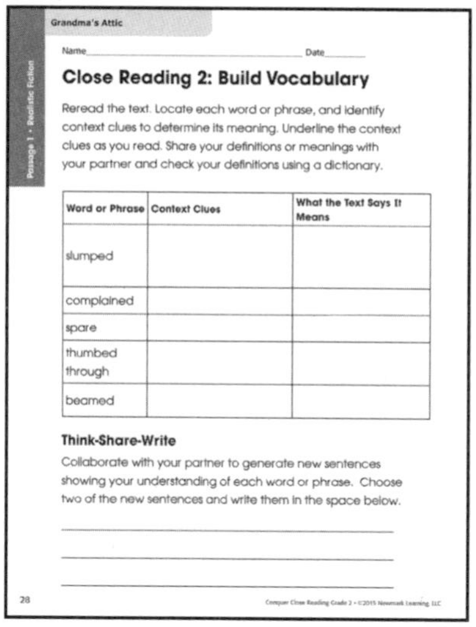

Grandma's Attic

Passage 1 • Realistic Fiction

Name________________ Date________

Close Reading 2: Build Vocabulary

Reread the text. Locate each word or phrase, and identify context clues to determine its meaning. Underline the context clues as you read. Share your definitions or meanings with your partner and check your definitions using a dictionary.

Word or Phrase	Context Clues	What the Text Says It Means
slumped		
complained		
spare		
thumbed through		
beamed		

Think-Share-Write

Collaborate with your partner to generate new sentences showing your understanding of each word or phrase. Choose two of the new sentences and write them in the space below.

28 Conquer Close Reading Grade 2 • ©2015 Newmark Learning, LLC

Step 3

The third reading centers on text structure. For informational texts, one of the five basic patterns of text structure is explored, giving students an opportunity to explore the relationship between meaning and text structure. For literary texts, the focus is on how basic story elements interact to bring life to a work of fiction.

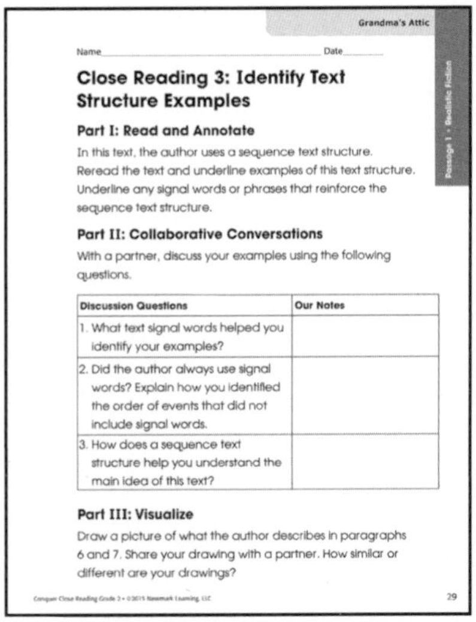

Grandma's Attic

Passage 1 • Realistic Fiction

Name_____________ Date_______

Close Reading 3: Identify Text Structure Examples

Part I: Read and Annotate

In this text, the author uses a sequence text structure. Reread the text and underline examples of this text structure. Underline any signal words or phrases that reinforce the sequence text structure.

Part II: Collaborative Conversations

With a partner, discuss your examples using the following questions.

Discussion Questions	Our Notes
1. What text signal words helped you identify your examples?	
2. Did the author always use signal words? Explain how you identified the order of events that did not include signal words.	
3. How does a sequence text structure help you understand the main idea of this text?	

Part III: Visualize

Draw a picture of what the author describes in paragraphs 6 and 7. Share your drawing with a partner. How similar or different are your drawings?

Conquer Close Reading Grade 2 • ©2015 Newmark Learning, LLC 29

Step 4

The fourth reading focuses directly on the deeper meaning of text. Students make inferences, draw conclusions, and synthesize what a text tells them; consider the broader implications of textual information; and consider the author's purpose and point of view.

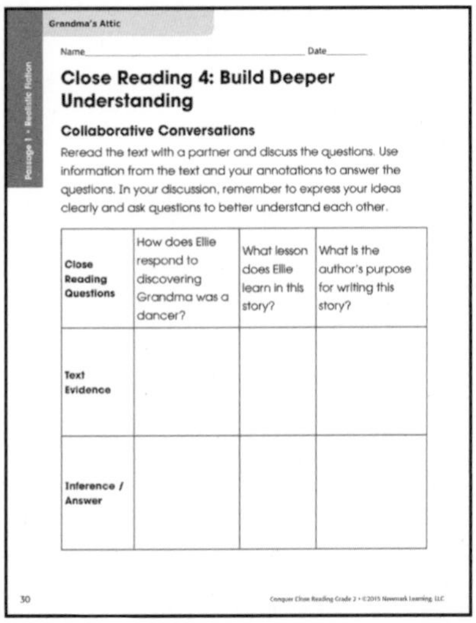

Grandma's Attic

Passage 1 • Realistic Fiction

Name_____________ Date_______

Close Reading 4: Build Deeper Understanding

Collaborative Conversations

Reread the text with a partner and discuss the questions. Use information from the text and your annotations to answer the questions. In your discussion, remember to express your ideas clearly and ask questions to better understand each other.

Close Reading Questions	How does Ellie respond to discovering Grandma was a dancer?	What lesson does Ellie learn in this story?	What is the author's purpose for writing this story?
Text Evidence			
Inference / Answer			

30 Conquer Close Reading Grade 2 • ©2015 Newmark Learning, LLC

Step 5

Finally, students have an opportunity to write about what they've read. First they analyze a writing prompt based on the text so they know exactly what is expected in their written response. Then they use their annotations, discussion notes, and text evidence as they write a narrative, informative/explanatory, or opinion/argument piece in response to the prompt.

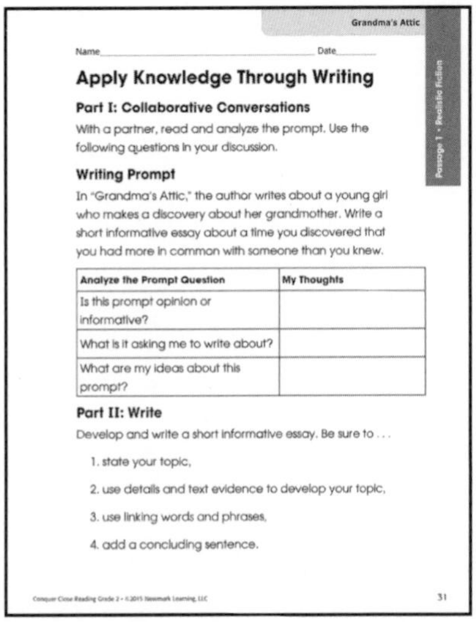

Grandma's Attic

Passage 1 • Realistic Fiction

Name_____________ Date_______

Apply Knowledge Through Writing

Part I: Collaborative Conversations

With a partner, read and analyze the prompt. Use the following questions in your discussion.

Writing Prompt

In "Grandma's Attic," the author writes about a young girl who makes a discovery about her grandmother. Write a short informative essay about a time you discovered that you had more in common with someone than you knew.

Analyze the Prompt Question	My Thoughts
Is this prompt opinion or informative?	
What is it asking me to write about?	
What are my ideas about this prompt?	

Part II: Write

Develop and write a short informative essay. Be sure to . . .

1. state your topic,
2. use details and text evidence to develop your topic,
3. use linking words and phrases,
4. add a concluding sentence.

Conquer Close Reading Grade 2 • ©2015 Newmark Learning, LLC 31

Using the Bonus Tools and Resources

Sentence Resource

The end of each grade-level volume of Conquer Close Reading features resources for students and teachers alike. There is a page of additional sentence frames that students can use during their collaborative conversations.

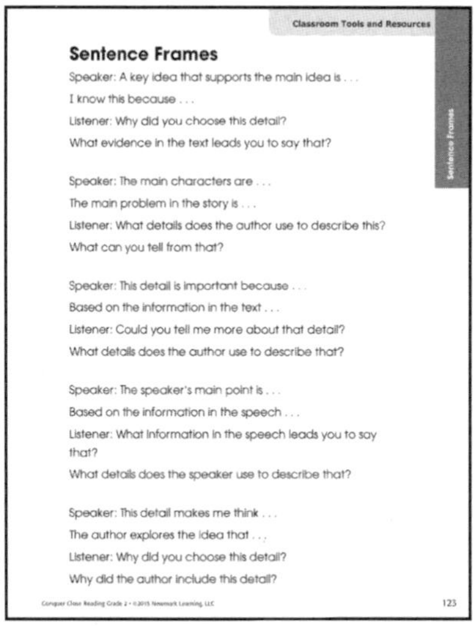

Classroom Tools and Resources

Sentence Frames

Sentence Frames

Speaker: A key idea that supports the main idea is . . .
I know this because . . .
Listener: Why did you choose this detail?
What evidence in the text leads you to say that?

Speaker: The main characters are . . .
The main problem in the story is . . .
Listener: What details does the author use to describe this?
What can you tell from that?

Speaker: This detail is important because . . .
Based on the information in the text . . .
Listener: Could you tell me more about that detail?
What details does the author use to describe that?

Speaker: The speaker's main point is . . .
Based on the information in the speech . . .
Listener: What information in the speech leads you to say that?
What details does the speaker use to describe that?

Speaker: This detail makes me think . . .
The author explores the idea that . . .
Listener: Why did you choose this detail?
Why did the author include this detail?

Conquer Close Reading Grade 2 • ©2015 Newmark Learning, LLC 123

Writing Checklists

Following the sentence frames are three writing checklists—one each for narrative writing, informative/explanatory writing, and opinion/argument writing. The checklists can be used by students to check their own writing or to conduct peer evaluation. Teachers can also use the checklists to monitor students' progress in developing writing skills.

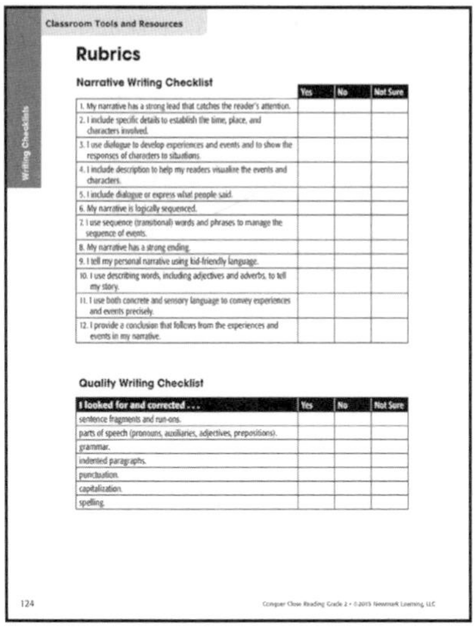

Classroom Tools and Resources

Writing Checklists

Rubrics

Narrative Writing Checklist

	Yes	No	Not Sure
1. My narrative has a strong lead that catches the reader's attention.			
2. I include specific details to establish the time, place, and characters involved.			
3. I use dialogue to develop experiences and events and to show the responses of characters to situations.			
4. I include description to help my readers visualize the events and characters.			
5. I include dialogue or express what people said.			
6. My narrative is logically sequenced.			
7. I use sequence (transitional) words and phrases to manage the sequence of events.			
8. My narrative has a strong ending.			
9. I tell my personal narrative using kid-friendly language.			
10. I use describing words, including adjectives and adverbs, to tell my story.			
11. I use both concrete and sensory language to convey experiences and events precisely.			
12. I provide a conclusion that follows from the experiences and events in my narrative.			

Quality Writing Checklist

I looked for and corrected . . .	Yes	No	Not Sure
sentence fragments and run-ons.			
parts of speech (pronouns, auxiliaries, adjectives, prepositions).			
grammar.			
indented paragraphs.			
punctuation.			
capitalization.			
spelling.			

124 Conquer Close Reading Grade 2 • ©2015 Newmark Learning, LLC

Building Block Mini-Lessons with Model Texts

Mini-Lesson 1: Monitor Your Reading

Objectives: In this mini-lesson, students will:

- monitor their reading
- use fix-up strategies (reread and talk about the text)

Materials:

- Model Text 2: "Keep Orcas Free," pages 21–22

Introduce

Explain that remembering details about what we read isn't always easy. Sometimes we get to the end of the text and can't remember what the text is about. Tell students that today they will learn two fix-up strategies to use when this happens.

Model

Display Model Text 2 and read the first paragraph. **Say:** *Now that I've read this paragraph, I ask myself, "What are a few details from this paragraph?" If I can't name a few details, I use two strategies to help me. First, I reread the paragraph and look for details. Second, I say the details I find aloud or in my head to remember them. I can also talk with a friend about the text to help me understand and remember it.*

Reread the first paragraph. While rereading, stop and repeat important details.

After sentence 3, **say:** *Orcas are also called killer whales. I think I knew that.*

After sentence 5, **say:** *So orcas leap into the air and land with a splash. They also push trainers around on their noses. I'd like to be a trainer.*

After the last sentence, **say:** *Oh! Parks are bad for whales. I wonder why.*

Remind students that rereading and talking about the text will help them remember what they read.

Practice

In pairs, have students read Model Text 2, paragraph 2. Encourage them to talk about the text with their partner as they reread.

Share and Discuss

Invite students to share thoughts and ideas about the text. Ask students how rereading and talking about the text helped them remember what they read.

Mini-Lesson 2: Identify and Annotate Key Details and Main Ideas

Objectives: In this mini-lesson, students will:

- identify key details
- determine main ideas

Materials:

- Model Text 2: "Keep Orcas Free," pages 21–22

Introduce

Remind students that most details in a paragraph are about one idea. This idea is called the main idea of the paragraph. Tell students that today they will learn to put details together to find a main idea.

Model

Display Model Text 2 and read paragraph 2. **Say:** *Now that I've read this paragraph, I ask myself, "What are the details mostly about?" Watch me as I analyze the text. Analyzing means studying closely. Then I will annotate the text to answer my questions. Annotating means highlighting important parts of the text and taking notes about them.*

Reread paragraph 2. Then identify and annotate key details to determine the main idea of the paragraph. **Say:** *The first sentence says that many whales have been taken from their ocean home. I'll highlight "taken from their ocean home." The second sentence says the tanks are not natural. I'll highlight "tanks" and "not natural." The third sentence says tanks are not like the ocean. I'll highlight "not" and "big, open ocean full of fish."* Model highlighting the text. Repeat with the remaining sentences.

Sentences 4 and 5—live in pods with 15–40 whales in each pod
Sentence 6—spend entire lives in the same pod with their mother
Sentences 7, 8, and 9—swim 100 miles a day, hunt together, have own language

Say: *So what are those details all about? I think this paragraph is about the difference between life in a tank and life in the ocean. This is the main idea.* Model writing this main idea to the side of paragraph 2.

Remind students that identifying and annotating key details helps them determine main ideas.

Practice

In pairs, have students read Model Text 2, paragraph 4. Encourage partners to identify and annotate key details and determine a main idea.

Share and Discuss

Ask students to explain how they identified and annotated key details and determined a main idea.

Mini-Lesson 3: Annotate and Analyze Setting

Objectives: In this mini-lesson, students will:

- identify important details about setting
- annotate important details about setting

Materials:

- Model Text 1: "Russian River Adventure," pages 19–20

Introduce

Remind students that authors include clues that tell the setting, or when and where a story takes place. Tell students that today they will learn to identify and annotate important details about the setting.

Model

Display Model Text 1 and read paragraph 1. **Say:** *I can tell who this story is about and what they were going to do. But what does the paragraph say about where and when the story happened? Watch as I annotate the text to answer my question.*

Reread the first paragraph and **say:** *I see where the story takes place. Harmony and her dad are riding bicycles heading toward the Russian River. I'll highlight "bicycle," "riding to the Russian River," and "path." Next, I'll write "where" along the side of paragraph 1 and write "on bicycles on a path to the Russian River."* Model writing the setting beside the paragraph.

Remind students to look for and annotate clues that tell the setting.

Practice

In pairs, have students reread the first paragraph. Encourage partners to identify the "when" in the story. Students should focus on clues that suggest time of day. (Example: "They were heading to the Russian River to swim and picnic. The sun was like a ball of fire in the sky. It had rained the night before, too . . . Harmony was already tired." Evidence suggests time of day is late morning or early afternoon.)

Share and Discuss

Invite students to share thoughts and ideas about the text. Ask students to explain how they annotated the text to analyze when the story takes place.

Mini-Lesson 4: Identify and Annotate Key Words and Phrases

Objectives: In this mini-lesson, students will:

- identify key words
- identify and annotate direct definitions of key words

Materials:

- Model Text 2: "Keep Orcas Free," pages 21–22

Introduce

Remind students that authors often tell the meaning of unfamiliar words directly in the text. These are called direct definitions. Tell students that today they will learn how to identify and annotate direct definitions of unfamiliar words.

Model

Write the following sentences on chart paper or the whiteboard.

1. "Jimmy and Donna quarreled, or argued, so much that their mother sent them to their rooms."
2. "Red-hot melted rock called magma comes out of a volcano."

Say: *In the first sentence, the author tells me what the word* ***quarreled*** *means by providing a direct definition. The author uses a comma and the word "or" to show a familiar word, "argued," which means the same thing as quarreled. I'll highlight "quarreled, or argued" to remember what* ***quarreled*** *means.* Model highlighting the text. *In the second sentence, the author tells me what the word* ***magma*** *means. The author describes a thing, "red-hot melted rock" and then uses the word "called" to make a definition. This tells us that red-hot melted rock is also called magma. I'll highlight "red-hot melted rock called magma" to remember what* ***magma*** *means.* Model highlighting the text.

Remind students to look for direct definitions when they read to help them define unfamiliar words.

Practice

In pairs, have students reread Model Text 2, paragraphs 1 and 2. Encourage students to identify and annotate direct definitions that help them define *orcas* and *pods*.

Share and Discuss

Invite students to share thoughts and ideas about the text. Ask students to explain how they identified and annotated direct definitions of the unfamiliar words.

Mini-Lesson 5: Identify Important Story Events to Use in a Summary

Objectives: In this mini-lesson, students will:

- identify and annotate important events to use in a summary

Materials:

- Model Text 1: "Russian River Adventure," pages 19–20

Introduce

Remind students that stories are made up of events that happen in a certain order. We retell the story using the order, or sequence, of events. When we retell just the most important events, we give a summary. Tell students that today they will learn how to identify and annotate the most important events to use in a summary.

Model

Display Model Text 1 and read paragraphs 1 through 6. **Say:** *Now I'll reread the paragraphs to find important events. Watch as I do this.*

Reread paragraphs 1 through 6. After reading, stop and annotate important events. **Say:** *The first important event is the beginning of the story. Harmony is riding to Russian River with her dad. I'll highlight "Harmony," "Dad," and "riding to the Russian River."* Model highlighting the text, then **say:** *The rest of this paragraph describes what the day was like. Those are not events. They are descriptions.*

Say: *The second paragraph is the next important event. They arrive at the river, but Dad is not happy. I'll highlight that whole paragraph.* Model highlighting the text and **say:** *The next two paragraphs are events, but they are not important. They are dialogue that makes the story move along. Paragraphs 5 and 6 are important events, though. They show why Dad is not happy.* Model highlighting the text and **say:** *When I'm ready to write a summary, I will use only the important events.*

Remind students that identifying and understanding the important events in a story will help them write a strong summary.

Practice

In pairs, have students reread the rest of the story. Encourage partners to identify and annotate the important events in paragraphs 7–12.

Share and Discuss

Invite students to share thoughts and ideas about the text. Ask students to explain how they identified and annotated the important events.

Mini-Lesson 6: Annotate and Determine Text Structure and Organization

Objectives: In this mini-lesson, students will:

- deconstruct a topic-and-facts text structure and organization
- annotate a topic-and-facts text structure and organization

Materials:

- Model Text 2: "Keep Orcas Free," pages 21–22

Introduce

Explain to students that authors write in patterns. These patterns are also called text structures. It is easier to understand what an author is saying if we understand the pattern. Tell students that today they will learn how authors use a topic-and-facts pattern, or text structure, to organize information.

Model

Display Model Text 2 and read paragraph 1. **Say:** *I can tell that the author is mostly using a topic-and-fact text structure in this paragraph. Watch as I model how I know.*

Reread the first two sentences of paragraph 1 and **say:** *A topic is what a paragraph is mostly about. These first two sentences tell me the topic of this paragraph. The topic is why people go to water parks. They go to watch sea animals do tricks. I'll write the topic to the side of the paragraph.* Model annotating the text.

Reread sentences 3 through 6 and **say:** *These sentences are facts about the topic sentences. Facts help support the topic sentence. I'll put a big **F** for **fact** at the beginning of each of these sentences.* Model annotating the text.

Reread sentence 7 and **say:** *This last sentence isn't really a fact that supports the topic for this paragraph. Instead, this sentence tells an important point about water parks. They are not good for whales. I think this sentence might be the BIG TOPIC. The BIG TOPIC is what the whole text is about. All the paragraphs support the BIG TOPIC. I'll underline that sentence.* Model highlighting the text. Remind students that annotating a text's structure will help them better understand the text.

Practice

In pairs, have students read Model Text 2, paragraph 3. Encourage students to identify and annotate the topic sentence and supporting facts for this paragraph.

Share and Discuss

Invite students to share their thoughts and ideas about the text. Ask students to explain how they identified and annotated the topic sentence and supporting facts.

Mini-Lesson 7: Analyze Opinion/ Argument Prompts

Objectives: In this mini-lesson, students will:

- read and analyze opinion/argument prompts

Materials:

- Mini-Lesson Resources, Opinion/Argument Prompts 1 and 2, page 23

Introduce

Explain to students that the word *prompt* means "question." We must look at a prompt carefully so we can answer the question. Tell students that today they will learn how to analyze an opinion/argument prompt so they can write a strong answer that explains what they think.

Model

Display and read aloud Opinion/Argument Prompt 1. **Say:** *Now that I've read the prompt for the first time, I need to make sure I understand the vocabulary and content words. For example, the word* ***risk*** *means "a dangerous chance." In other words, you don't know what will happen, but it could turn out badly.*

Next, reread each sentence of the prompt. **Say:** *The first sentence explains the topic. I will be writing about Dad swimming out into the fast-moving water to save a puppy. The second sentence tells me exactly what I'm to write about. Do I think that Dad did the right thing? So, I am supposed to give my opinion about what Dad did. The last sentence tells me that I need to use information, or evidence, from the text to support my opinion. So I need to look through the text and find evidence that supports what I believe.*

Remind students that analyzing a prompt will help them write a strong answer to the question.

Practice

In pairs, have students read Opinion/Argument Prompt 2. Encourage students to analyze the prompt.

Share and Discuss

Invite students to share their thoughts and ideas about the prompt. Ask students to explain how they analyzed the prompt.

Mini-Lesson 8: Analyze Informative/ Explanatory Prompts

Objectives: In this mini-lesson, students will:

- read and analyze an informative/explanatory prompt

Materials:

- Mini-Lesson Resources, Informative/Explanatory Prompts 1 and 2, page 23

Introduce

Explain to students that the word *prompt* means "question." We must look at a prompt carefully so we can answer the question. Tell students that today they will learn how to analyze an informative/explanatory prompt so they can write a strong answer that explains the text.

Model

Display and read aloud Informative/Explanatory Prompt 1. **Say:** *Now that I've read the prompt for the first time, I need to make sure I understand the vocabulary and content words. For example, the word* ***compared*** *tells me that the author looked at killer whales two ways: both inside and outside of water parks.*

Next, reread each sentence of the prompt. **Say:** *The first sentence explains what the author wrote about. He wrote about what life is like for killer whales in water parks and in the ocean. The second sentence tells me what I'm supposed to write about. I'm asked to write about the bad things that happen to whales once they are brought to a water park. The last sentence tells me that I need to use information, or evidence, from the text to support my explanation. I won't need information from every paragraph. Paragraph 1 is about what people watch killer whales do in a water park. Paragraph 2 is about their lives in the ocean. Paragraphs 3 and 4 are about the bad, or negative, things that happen to whales in water parks. So it looks like I will only need information from paragraphs 3 and 4.*

Remind students that analyzing a prompt will help them write a strong answer to the question.

Practice

In pairs, have students read Informative/Explanatory Prompt 2. Encourage students to analyze the prompt.

Share and Discuss

Invite students to share their thoughts and ideas about the prompt. Ask students to explain how they analyzed the prompt.

Mini-Lesson 9: Analyze Narrative Prompts

Objectives: In this mini-lesson, students will:

- read and analyze a narrative prompt

Materials:

- Mini-Lesson Resources, Narrative Prompts 1 and 2, page 23

Introduce

Explain to students that the word *prompt* means "question." We must look at a prompt carefully so we can answer the question. Tell students that today they will learn how to analyze a narrative prompt so they can write a story that answers the question.

Model

Display and read aloud Narrative Prompt 1. **Say:** *Now that I've read the prompt for the first time, I need to make sure I understand the vocabulary and content words. For example, the word **doomed** means "having no hope of survival." The puppy was probably going to drown if Dad did not save it.*

Next, reread each sentence of the prompt. **Say:** *The first sentence tells what the story is about with a really short summary. The second sentence tells what I'm to write about. It looks like I'm going to continue the story by telling how Harmony and her dad explained the puppy to Mom. The last sentence tells me to use events from the story in my own story. Well, if I'm writing about the puppy, I don't need to give a lot of information about the journey to the river. I need to start where they found the puppy and tell how Dad jumped into the water to save it. I need to include that Dad knew he could do it because he was a champion swimmer. I should probably use the word **careful** as many times as possible, or Mom may never let those two out of the house again!*

Remind students that analyzing a prompt will help them write a strong short story that answers the question.

Practice

In pairs, have students read Narrative Prompt 2. Encourage students to analyze the prompt.

Share and Discuss

Invite students to share their thoughts and ideas about the prompt. Ask students to explain how they analyzed the prompt.

Mini-Lesson 10: Choose Text Evidence That Supports the Prompt

Objectives: In this mini-lesson, students will:

- identify text evidence that supports the writer's answer to a prompt

Materials:

- Model Text 2: "Keep Orcas Free," pages 21–22
- Mini-Lesson Resources, Narrative Prompt 2, page 23

Introduce

Explain to students that when they are writing to a prompt, they must include evidence from the text that supports their answer. Tell students that today they will learn how to identify text evidence that best supports their ideas.

Model

Display and read Narrative Prompt 2. **Say:** *This prompt is interesting because I will be using a nonfiction text to write a story. The trick is to turn facts into fiction. An easy way to do this is to write diary entries that sound like a whale wrote them. I need to review the text and decide which evidence or facts I want to use in my diary entries.*

Display Model Text 2 and **say:** *I am supposed to write about a whale's life in the water park. I'll start by looking for information about this topic. Paragraph 3 explains what life is like in a water park, and it doesn't sound very fun.* Read paragraph 3 and **say:** *In my first diary entry, I could write that I miss my mother and family and that I can't talk to anybody because they speak a different language from me.* Model highlighting paragraph 3, sentences 2 and 3. **Say:** *In the next entry, I could write about how small these tanks are and that the fish taste terrible. I could add that I don't even get to hunt.* Model highlighting information from sentences 4 through 6. *The information in paragraph 3 definitely helps me write a story from a captured whale's point of view.*

Remind students that identifying text evidence that answers the prompt will help them write a strong narrative.

Practice

Invite students to share their thoughts and ideas. Ask students to explain how they identified text evidence to add to their narrative.

Share and Discuss

Invite students to share their thoughts and ideas. Ask students to explain how they identified text evidence to support the answer to the prompt.

Mini-Lesson 11: Collaborative Conversations: Speaker Expresses Clear Ideas

Objectives: In this mini-lesson, students will:

- use sentence frames to organize thoughts

Materials:

- Model Text 1: "Russian River Adventure," pages 19–20
- Mini-Lesson Resources, Sentence Frames for Organizing Ideas, page 23

Introduce

Remind students that everyone has ideas and wants to express them, but they can be difficult to understand. Sometimes people don't stay focused. They talk about a lot of things. Sentence frames can keep our thoughts organized. Tell students that today they will learn how to use sentence frames to organize their thoughts so they can clearly express their ideas.

Model

Display Model Text 1. Read paragraph 3. **Say:** *Now that I've read the text, I need to decide what I think and how to say it. I'll look at my sentence frames.* Display and read Sentence Frames for Organizing Ideas. **Say:** *I'll use the first frame for my thought.* Model saying the thought using the frame: *I think that Harmony is not having a very good time.* **Say:** *Now I'll use the other frames to help me organize my thoughts. When I use evidence from the text, I name the paragraph or sentence.* Model organizing evidence using sentence frames. **Say:** *In sentence 2, the author says Harmony was having a tough time keeping up with Dad. Later in the paragraph, the author adds that the air was heavy and Harmony was already tired. This really doesn't sound like much fun.*

Remind students to organize their ideas using sentence frames before they speak, so everyone can understand them.

Practice

In pairs, have students reread Model Text 1, paragraph 10. Ask them to discuss Dad's attitude toward saving the puppy and jumping into the fast river. Encourage students to use the sentence frames form to express their thoughts. Then ask students to practice speaking clearly to each other.

Share and Discuss

Invite students to share answers and text evidence. Ask students to explain what they learned from this activity about using sentence frames to organize ideas.

Mini-Lesson 12: Collaborative Conversations: Listener Asks Questions

Objectives: In this mini-lesson, students will:

- ask questions to understand

Materials:

- Model Text 1: "Russian River Adventure," pages 19–20
- Mini-Lesson Resources, Ask Questions Anchor Chart, page 23

Introduce

Remind students that it isn't always easy to understand what someone is saying. Sometimes, speakers do not stay focused on one topic. Tell students that today they will ask questions to help them understand what is being said.

Model

Display Model Text 1. Read paragraphs 8, 9, and 10. **Say:** *Pretend I am the speaker. I'm going to tell one thought I have about Harmony from the information in these paragraphs. I don't think she was worried about her dad. Doesn't she know how dangerous this is?* Explain to students that you did not offer a clear thought based on the text. You gave your thought and added a question. **Say:** *When we are confused about what a speaker says, we should ask a few simple questions. Here are some questions you can ask when you don't understand.*

Display Ask Questions Anchor Chart. Tell students to ask one or more of these questions if they are confused. Invite a student to ask you one of these questions. **Say:** *Oh, yes. My answer was not very focused. I should have said that Harmony really didn't have time to worry about her father. Harmony said they had to save the puppy. Dad agreed, and then he jumped into the water. Does that make more sense to everyone?*

Remind students to ask questions when they don't understand what is being said.

Practice

Reread paragraphs 1 through 7. Tell students that these paragraphs lead you to think that Harmony doesn't like to bike. In pairs, have students consider what part of this idea is confusing and what questions they would ask to understand your idea better. Then, encourage pairs to come up with their own ideas about Harmony based on information from the text. Remind them to provide text evidence that supports their ideas.

Share and Discuss

Invite students to share their questions and ideas about Harmony and about the evidence that supports their ideas.

Name______________________________ Date__________

Model Text 1: Realistic Fiction

Russian River Adventure

by Patrick Mulvihill

1 Harmony pushed hard on her bicycle pedals. It was tough to keep up with Dad. They were riding on a path to the Russian River to swim and picnic. The sun was like a ball of fire in the sky. It had rained the night before, too, so the air was very heavy. Harmony was already tired.

2 Finally, they arrived at the river. Harmony cheered, but Dad frowned.

3 "What's wrong?" she asked.

4 "All that rain last night made the river run fast. Look," replied Dad.

5 The water was very high. It was rushing like a train. It crashed against the bank. A stick in the water flew past and hit a rock. The stick snapped in two.

6 "I'm sorry, but it's way too dangerous to swim," said Dad.

continued

Name____ Date__________

7 "So we rode all this way for nothing?" complained Harmony. "This is the worst day ever!"

8 Suddenly, they heard a strange noise, like a baby crying or a dog barking. Then, they saw a puppy trapped on a rock in the middle of the river.

9 "Oh, no! We have to save him!" Harmony shouted.

10 "We don't have any choice, do we? He's in trouble!" Dad said. Dad had been a champion swimmer when he was younger. He ran and dove into the swift river. Dad disappeared underwater. Then, all of a sudden, he popped up beside the puppy. The scared little creature jumped into Dad's arms. He swam back to the bank.

11 "It's not the worst day after all, is it?" asked Dad. He handed the puppy to Harmony.

12 "Who needs to swim, anyway?" she laughed as the wet puppy licked her nose.

Name____ Date__________

Model Text 2: Science Essay
Keep Orcas Free

by Patrick Mulvihill

1 Every year, millions of people go to water parks. They go to watch sea animals do tricks. The most famous of all the animal performers are the orcas, or killer whales. These whales leap high into the air and land with a splash. They also push their human trainers around the water with their noses. It is a very fun show. But most people don't know that these parks are bad for the whales.

2 Many of the whales have been taken from their ocean home. The tanks where whales live in a park are not natural. They are not a big, open ocean full of fish. In the wild, orcas live in family groups called pods. These pods have anywhere from 15 to 40 whales in them. Orcas spend their entire lives in their pod with their mother. They swim up to 100 miles a day. They hunt together. They even have their own language.

continued

Name____ Date_________

3 All of these things change once the orcas live in a water park. They are no longer with their mothers or families. They live with strange whales that speak different languages. In the small tanks, they cannot swim 100 miles in a day. They no longer hunt. They are fed fish instead of hunting them. Orcas also do not live as long in these tanks.

4 All of this is very bad for the whales. They often become sick with diseases that they don't get in the ocean. They sometimes even bite people, which is something they never do in the wild. People might tell you we need orcas to live in parks so we can learn more about them. But it is better to study them in the wild. In the ocean we can see their natural behavior. In the ocean they can be healthy and free.

Mini-Lesson Resources

Opinion/Argument Prompt 1

In "Russian River Adventure," Dad risks his life to save the puppy. Do you think he did the right thing? In your answer, give your opinion and at least two reasons for your opinion. Support your opinion with evidence from the text.

Opinion/Argument Prompt 2

In "Keep Orcas Free," the author explains why water parks are bad for killer whales. Do you agree or disagree with the author? In your answer, give your opinion and at least two reasons for your opinion. Support your opinion with evidence from the text.

Informative/Explanatory Prompt 1

In "Keep Orcas Free," the author describes how life is different for a killer whale in a water park as compared with the ocean. After rereading the text, write a short essay that explains the bad things that happen to whales once they are brought to a water park. Support your writing with evidence from the text.

Informative/Explanatory Prompt 2

After reading "Keep Orcas Free," write a short essay that explains why the author thinks living in the ocean is better for killer whales. Support your writing with evidence from the text.

Narrative Prompt 1

In "Russian River Adventure," Harmony and her father go on an exciting adventure and save a doomed animal. After reading the story, write a short narrative about what happened after they got home. How did they explain the puppy to Harmony's mom? Use events from the story in your narrative.

Narrative Prompt 2

In "Keep Orcas Free," the author describes a killer whale's life in a water park. After reading the article, write a short story in which you pretend you are a killer whale who has been captured and brought to a water park. Describe what your new life is like. Include information from the article in your story.

Sentence Frames for Organizing Ideas

1. I think __________________.
2. In sentence _____, _____________ says ______________________.
3. In paragraph ____________, __________________ happens.

Ask Questions Anchor Chart

Questions to Help My Understanding

1. What did you mean when you said _________________?
2. So, do you mean ___________________?
3. What evidence from the text makes you think that way?

Table of Contents

Literary Passages

Informational Passages

Name____________________ Date________

Passage 1: Realistic Fiction

Grandma's Attic

by Michelle Olmsted

1 Ellie slumped on her grandmother's couch. She was not happy about spending the whole weekend at Grandma's house. "It's so boring there," she had complained to her parents. "There's nothing to do!"

2 Grandma walked in from the kitchen. "Do you want to play cards?"

3 "Not really," Ellie sighed. "I think I'll just do my homework."

4 "Okay," said Grandma. "I'll be in the kitchen. Holler if you need me."

5 Ellie dragged her backpack down the hall to the spare bedroom. A staircase from the ceiling blocked the bedroom door. Ellie let the straps of her backpack drop to the floor. She had never been in Grandma's attic before. She quietly climbed the stairs.

6 The small attic space was lined with boxes and clothes racks. A ruffled skirt caught Ellie's attention. She thumbed

continued

Name________________________________ Date__________

through the racks of sequined skirts and pale pink tutus. She took one of the tutus off the hanger and pulled it up over her jeans. She twisted from side to side.

7 Ellie imagined what it would be like to be a ballerina, dancing across a stage. Suddenly, a noise startled Ellie out of her daydream.

8 "Well, don't you look beautiful in my old tutu," Grandma said at the top of the stairs.

9 "This is yours?" Ellie asked. "I didn't know you were a dancer."

10 "I sure was," Grandma said. "A pretty good one, too!"

11 "I want to be a dancer someday," said Ellie. "I take ballet classes after school."

12 "Let's bring these costumes downstairs, and you can try them all on," Grandma said.

13 Ellie beamed. "I have an idea. We can put on a show!"

14 "Now, that sounds like fun!" Grandma said.

Name____ Date__________

Close Reading 1: Read for Story Elements

"Grandma's Attic" is mostly about a young girl who makes a discovery about her grandmother while exploring her attic. Read the story and underline its key elements. Then complete the graphic organizer using details from the story.

Story Map

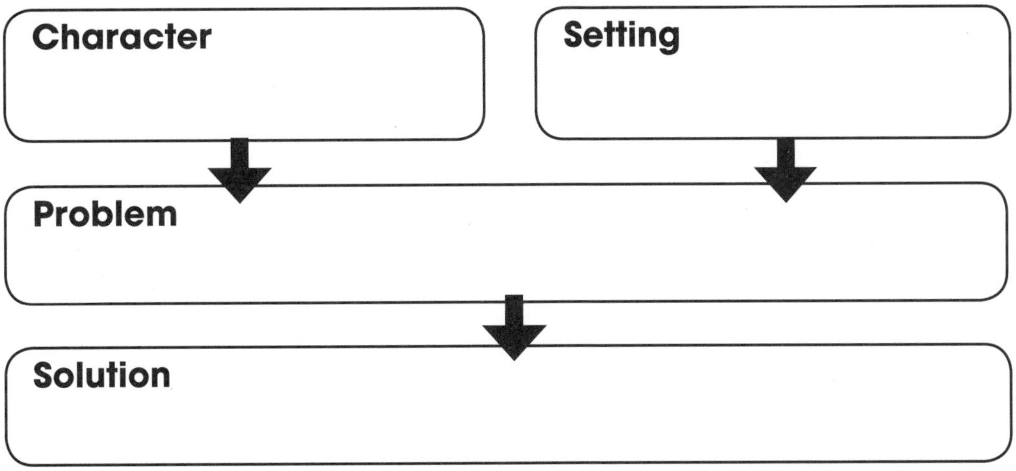

Collaborative Conversations

Discuss your answers with a partner. When you speak, state what your ideas tell about the story elements. When you listen, ask questions to clarify what the speaker says.

Sentence Frames:

Speaker: The main problem of the story is . . .

I know this because . . .

Listener: Why do you think that?

What details does the author use to describe that?

Name____ Date__________

Close Reading 2: Build Vocabulary

Reread the text. Locate each word or phrase, and identify context clues to determine its meaning. Underline the context clues as you read. Share your definitions or meanings with your partner and check your definitions using a dictionary.

Word or Phrase	Context Clues	What the Text Says It Means
slumped		
complained		
spare		
thumbed through		
beamed		

Think-Share-Write

Collaborate with your partner to generate new sentences showing your understanding of each word or phrase. Choose two of the new sentences and write them in the space below.

____

____

____

Name_______________________________________ Date_________

Close Reading 3: Identify Text Structure Examples

Part I: Read and Annotate

In this text, the author uses a sequence text structure. Reread the text and underline examples of this text structure. Underline any signal words or phrases that reinforce the sequence text structure.

Part II: Collaborative Conversations

With a partner, discuss your examples using the following questions.

Discussion Questions	Our Notes
1. What text signal words helped you identify your examples?	
2. Did the author always use signal words? Explain how you identified the order of events that did not include signal words.	
3. How does a sequence text structure help you understand the main idea of this text?	

Part III: Visualize

Draw a picture of what the author describes in paragraphs 6 and 7. Share your drawing with a partner. How similar or different are your drawings?

Name____ Date__________

Close Reading 4: Build Deeper Understanding

Collaborative Conversations

Reread the text with a partner and discuss the questions. Use information from the text and your annotations to answer the questions. In your discussion, remember to express your ideas clearly and ask questions to better understand each other.

Close Reading Questions	How does Ellie respond to discovering Grandma was a dancer?	What lesson does Ellie learn in this story?	What is the author's purpose for writing this story?
Text Evidence			
Inference/ Answer			

Name____ Date__________

Apply Knowledge Through Writing

Part I: Collaborative Conversations

With a partner, read and analyze the prompt. Use the following questions in your discussion.

Writing Prompt

In "Grandma's Attic," the author writes about a young girl who makes a discovery about her grandmother. Write a short informative essay about a time you discovered that you had more in common with someone than you knew.

Analyze the Prompt Question	**My Thoughts**
Is this prompt opinion/argument or informative/explanatory?	
What is it asking me to write about?	
What are my ideas about this prompt?	

Part II: Write

Develop and write a short informative essay. Be sure to . . .

1. state your topic,
2. use details and text evidence to develop your topic,
3. use linking words and phrases,
4. add a concluding sentence.

Name____ Date__________

Passage 2: Poem

Popcorn

by Evaleen Stein

Pop! Pop!—Poppetty-pop!
Shake and rattle and rattle and shake
The golden grains as they bounce and break
To fluffy puffiness—*Poppetty-pop!*
Bursting and banging the popper's top!
Poppetty-pop!
Pop! Pop!
The yellow kernels, oh, see them grow
White as cotton or flakes of snow!
Pop! Pop!

Name______________________________ Date________

O-ho, how they frolic and fly about
And turn themselves suddenly inside out!
Pop-pop-poppetty! Pop-pop-pop!
The popper's full and we'll have to stop;
Pile the bowl with the tempting treat,
Children, come, it is time to eat!

Name____ Date__________

Close Reading 1: Read for Poetry Elements

"Popcorn" describes the sights and sounds of popping corn. Read the poem and underline the words that describe the popping corn. Think about how the author describes what she sees and hears. Then complete the graphic organizer, using the sensory details from the poem.

See	Hear

Collaborative Conversations

Discuss your answers with a partner. When you are the speaker, state your ideas and explain why you think these details help the reader imagine the popping corn. When you are the listener, ask questions to clarify what the speaker says.

Sentence Frames:

Speaker: The author's main point is . . .

A sensory detail that helps me imagine is . . .

Listener: Why did the author choose this detail to describe the popping corn?

What does this detail tell you?

Name______________________________ Date________

Close Reading 2: Build Vocabulary

Reread the text. Locate each word or phrase, and identify context clues to determine its meaning. Underline the context clues as you read. Share your definitions or meanings with your partner and check your definitions, using a dictionary.

Word or Phrase	Context Clues	What the Text Says It Means
rattle		
bursting		
kernels		
frolic		

Think-Share-Write

Collaborate with your partner to generate new sentences, showing your understanding of each word or phrase. Choose two of the new sentences and write them in the space below.

____

____

____

____

Name______________________________________ Date_________

Close Reading 3: Identify Text Structure Examples

Part I: Read and Annotate

In this text, the author mainly uses a descriptive text structure to create an image of popping corn. Reread the text and underline examples of this text structure. Underline signal words or phrases used that reinforce the text structure.

Part II: Collaborative Conversations

With a partner, discuss your examples using the following questions.

Discussion Questions	Our Notes
1. What text signal words helped you identify your examples?	
2. Did the author always use signal words? Explain how you identified a relationship that did not include signal words.	
3. How does a descriptive text structure help you understand the main idea of this text?	

Part III: Visualize

Draw a picture of what the author describes in the poem. Share your drawing with a partner. How similar or different are your drawings?

Name______________________________________ Date__________

Close Reading 4: Build Deeper Understanding

Collaborative Conversations

Reread the text with a partner and discuss the questions. Use information from the text and your ideas to answer the questions. In your discussion, remember to express your ideas clearly and ask questions to better understand each other.

Close Reading Questions	What comparisons does the author use to describe the popped corn?	How does the author create a cheerful mood?	What is the author's point of view about popcorn? How do you know?
Text Evidence	"		
Inference/ Answer			

Name____ Date__________

Apply Knowledge Through Writing

Part I: Collaborative Conversations

With a partner, read and analyze the prompt. Use the following questions in your discussion.

Writing Prompt

The author of "Popcorn" uses sensory details to describe the sights and sounds of popping corn. Write a rhyming poem that describes your favorite food or snack. Use sensory details that describe what you see, hear, feel, and smell.

Analyze the Prompt Question	My Thoughts
Is this prompt informative/ explanatory or narrative?	
What is it asking me to write about?	
What are my ideas about this prompt?	

Part II: Write

Develop and write a poem. Be sure to . . .

1. name your favorite food or snack,
2. follow an AABB rhyme pattern,
3. use a descriptive text structure,
4. use sensory details.

Name______________________________ Date________

Passage 3: Folktale
Anansi the Spider: A West African Folktale

West African; retold by Michelle Olmsted

1 Anansi was a sneaky spider. He often used tricks to get his way. But Anansi knew that tricks would not always work. He needed to be wise—wiser than everyone else.

2 Anansi asked his father, the sky god, to give him all of the world's wisdom. He promised he would share the wisdom. That was just a trick. He really wanted to keep the wisdom for himself.

3 The sneaky spider stored the wisdom in a large pot. *No one will be able to outsmart me!* he thought.

4 Anansi was afraid someone would find his pot. He looked for a good hiding spot. He decided to keep the pot in the highest branches of a tree.

5 Anansi knew that getting the pot up the tree would be difficult. He did not think to look in his pot of wisdom for an idea. Anansi thought he knew what to do. He tied the large pot to his belly.

continued

Name____ Date__________

The pot was so large his legs didn't reach the ground. He rolled from side to side, unable to get back on his feet.

6 Anansi's son looked on. He could not bear to see his father struggle. "Father," he said, "may I suggest you tie the pot to your back. That way, your legs will be free to grasp the tree."

7 Anansi was mad he had not thought of this idea himself. He quickly tied the pot to his back. Without a word to his son, Anansi climbed the tree.

8 His anger grew with each step. Anansi reached the top. He yelled up at the sky, "My son outsmarted me, and I have all of the wisdom!"

9 Anansi threw down the pot of wisdom. The pot fell to the ground. Tiny pieces of wisdom spread in every direction.

10 That is why one person does not hold all of the world's wisdom. Instead, wisdom is shared when people exchange ideas.

Name________________________ Date__________

Close Reading 1: Read for Story Elements

"Anansi the Spider" is mostly about a spider that tries to keep the world's wisdom for himself. Read the folktale and underline the key elements of the story. Then complete the graphic organizer using details from the folktale.

Story Map

Characters	**Setting**
Problem	**Solution**

Collaborative Conversations

Discuss your answers with a partner. When you speak, explain why you think your ideas tell about the story elements. When you listen, ask questions to clarify what the speaker says.

Sentence Frames:

Speaker: The author's main point is . . .

The author explores the idea that . . .

Listener: Why do you think that?

What details does the author use to describe that?

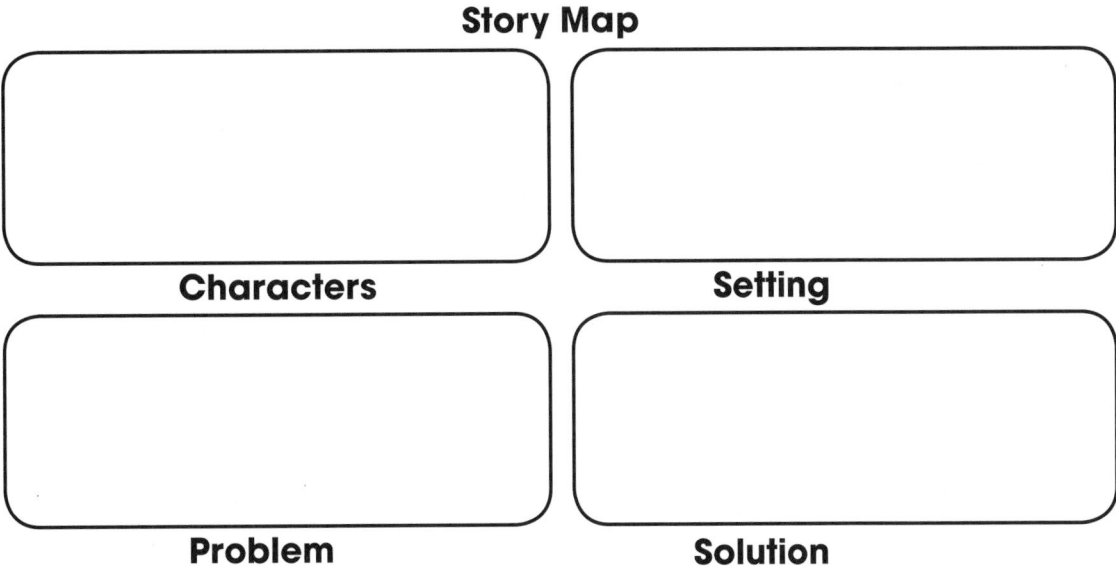

Name________________________________ Date__________

Close Reading 2: Build Vocabulary

Reread the text. Locate each word or phrase, and identify context clues to determine its meaning. Underline the context clues as you read. Share your definitions or meanings with your partner and check your definitions, using a dictionary.

Word or Phrase	**Context Clues**	**What the Text Says It Means**
wisdom		
stored		
bear		
exchange		

Think-Share-Write

Collaborate with your partner to generate new sentences showing your understanding of each word or phrase. Choose two of the new sentences and write them in the space below.

____

____

____

Name________________________________ Date__________

Close Reading 3: Identify Text Structure Examples

Part I: Read and Annotate

In this text, the author mainly uses a sequence text structure. Reread the text and underline examples of this text structure. Be sure to underline any signal words or phrases used by the author that reinforce the sequence text structure.

Part II: Collaborative Conversations

With a partner, discuss your examples using the following questions.

Discussion Questions	Our Notes
1. What text signal words helped you identify your examples?	
2. Did the author always use signal words? Explain how you identified the order of events without signal words.	
3. How does a sequence text structure help you understand the main idea?	

Part III: Visualize

Draw a picture of what the author describes in paragraph 5. Share your drawing with a partner. How similar or different are your drawings?

Name____________________________________ Date__________

Close Reading 4: Build Deeper Understanding

Collaborative Conversations

Reread the text with a partner and discuss the questions. Use information from the text and your ideas to answer the questions. In your discussion, remember to express your ideas clearly and ask questions to better understand each other.

Close Reading Questions	How does Anansi respond to his son's help? What does this tell you about Anansi's character?	What is the author's point of view about using tricks to get your way?	What is the author's purpose for writing this folktale?
Text Evidence			
Inference/ Answer			

Name______________________________ Date__________

Apply Knowledge Through Writing

Part I: Collaborative Conversations

With a partner, read and analyze the prompt. Use the following questions in your discussion.

Writing Prompt

In "Anansi the Spider," the author writes about a spider that tries to keep all of the world's wisdom for himself. Write a short story about different characters in a different setting that teaches a similar lesson about wisdom. Support your ideas with information from the folktale.

Analyze the Prompt Question	My Thoughts
Is this prompt opinion/argument or narrative?	
What is it asking me to write about?	
What are my ideas about this prompt?	

Part II: Write

Develop and write a short narrative. Be sure to:

1. develop the characters through actions and events,
2. use signal words showing time,
3. add an ending.

Name______________________________ Date________

Passage 4: Realistic Fiction
Why Minnie Could Not Sleep

by Dew Drops

1 Minnie sat up in bed. The curtain was open and she saw the moon. It looked as if it were laughing at her. "Don't look at me, Moon," she said. "You don't know about it. You can't even see in the daytime. I'm going to sleep."

2 She lay down and tried to sleep. Her clock went *tick-tock, tick-tock*. She usually liked to hear it, but tonight it sounded as if it said, "I know, I know, I know."

3 "You don't know, either," said Minnie, opening her eyes wide. "You weren't there, you old thing! You were upstairs."

4 Pretty soon there came a soft patter of four little feet. Minnie's cat jumped on the bed, kissed her cheek, and then began to purr. It was strange, but it sounded as if Kitty said, "I know, I know."

Name______________________________ Date________

5 "Yes, you do know, Kitty," said Minnie. She threw her arms around Kitty's neck and cried. "I guess I should go see Mamma!"

6 Mamma opened her eyes when she heard Minnie coming. Minnie told her the terrible story. "I was naughty, Mamma, but I wanted the apple pie so bad. So, I ate it up, almost the whole pie. Oh, I don't want to tell you, but I must. I shut Kitty in the pantry to make you think she did it. I'm truly sorry, Mamma."

7 Then Mamma told Minnie that she had known all about it. She had hoped that the little daughter would be brave enough to tell her about it herself.

8 "But Mamma," she asked, "how did you know it wasn't Kitty?"

9 "Because Kitty would never have left a spoon in the pie," replied Mamma, smiling.

Name____ Date__________

Close Reading 1: Read for Poetry Elements

"Why Minnie Could Not Sleep" is mostly about a young girl who learns a lesson about telling the truth. Read the realistic fiction and underline the key elements of the story. Then complete the graphic organizer using details from the story. You can add to the graphic organizer if necessary.

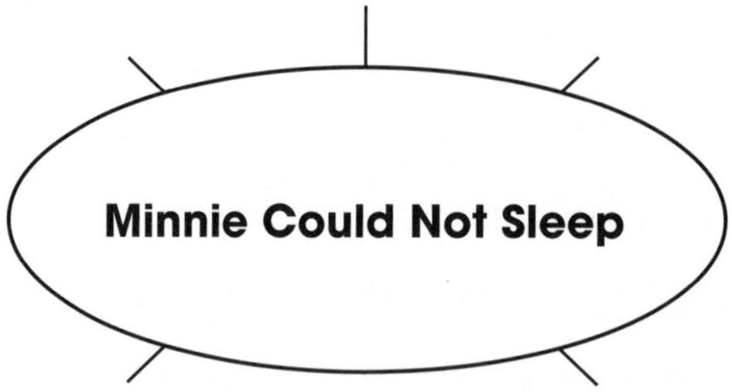

Collaborative Conversations

Discuss your answers with a partner. When you are the speaker, state your ideas and explain why you think they tell about why Minnie could not sleep. When you are the listener, ask questions to clarify what the speaker says.

Sentence Frames:

Speaker: The story focuses on . . .

The most important idea in the story is . . .

Listener: Could you tell me more about this idea?

What details does the author use to describe that?

Name____ Date__________

Close Reading 2: Build Vocabulary

Reread the text. Locate each word or phrase, and identify context clues to determine its meaning. Underline the context clues as you read. Share your definitions or meanings with your partner and check your definitions using a dictionary.

Word or Phrase	Context Clues	What the Text Says It Means
patter		
naughty		
pantry		
brave		

Think-Share-Write

Collaborate with your partner to generate new sentences. Show your understanding of each word or phrase. Choose two of the new sentences and write them in the space below.

____

____

____

Name_______________________________ Date__________

Close Reading 3: Identify Text Structure Examples

Part I: Read and Annotate

In this text, the author mainly uses a sequence text structure. Reread the text and underline examples of this text structure. Underline any signal words or phrases that reinforce the sequence text structure.

Part II: Collaborative Conversations

With a partner, discuss your examples using the following questions.

Discussion Questions	Our Notes
1. What signal words helped you identify your examples?	
2. Did the author always use signal words? Explain how you identified the order of events without signal words.	
3. How does a sequence text structure help you understand the main idea of this text?	

Part III: Visualize

Draw a picture of what the author describes in paragraphs 2 and 3. Share your drawing with a partner. How similar or different are your drawings?

Name______________________________ Date__________

Close Reading 4: Build Deeper Understanding

Collaborative Conversations

Reread the text with a partner and discuss the questions. Use information from the text and your ideas to answer the questions. In your discussion, remember to express your ideas clearly and ask questions to better understand each other.

Close Reading Questions	Why is Minnie unable to sleep?	When does Minnie first know Mamma found the pie?	What is the author's point of view about telling the truth?
Text Evidence		"	
Inference/ Answer			

Name________________________ Date________

Apply Knowledge Through Writing

Part I: Collaborative Conversations

With a partner, read and analyze the prompt. Use the following questions in your discussion.

Writing Prompt

In "Why Minnie Could Not Sleep," a young girl learns a lesson about telling the truth. Write a short essay that answers the following question: Do you think Minnie was brave to tell the truth? Support your opinion with information from the story.

Analyze the Prompt Question	My Thoughts
Is this prompt opinion/argument or narrative?	
What is it asking me to write about?	
What are my ideas about this prompt?	

Part II: Write

Develop and write a short opinion essay. Be sure to:

1. introduce your topic and state your opinion,
2. use text evidence for support,
3. use linking words and phrases that connect your opinion and reasons,
4. add a concluding sentence.

Name____ Date_________

Passage 5: Fable
Fox and Crow

retold by Michelle Olmsted

1 Fox was terribly hungry. He walked the forest looking for food. He spotted Crow flying with a piece of cheese in her beak. She landed on a branch of a nearby tree to eat her lunch.

2 *I shall get that cheese*, Fox said to himself as he walked toward Crow.

3 "Good day, Miss Crow," Fox called out. "Don't you look lovely today. Your feathers—they glisten! I don't think I have ever seen such shiny feathers on a crow. And your eyes—they are so bright. They sparkle in the sunlight."

4 Crow puffed out her feathers and batted her eyes.

5 "Without a doubt," continued Fox. "You are the most beautiful bird in the forest. I am sure you have the sweetest voice of all the birds, too. It would be such an honor to hear you sing just one song."

continued

Name______________________________ Date__________

6 Crow lifted her head to the sky. She closed her eyes and opened her mouth to caw her finest caw. But as soon as she did, the piece of cheese fell to the ground.

7 Fox snagged the cheese and gobbled it down. "Thank you, Crow," he said. "I prefer food to songs anyway. But as payment for your piece of cheese, I will give you a piece of advice. You should never trust a flatterer."

Name_______________________________________ Date__________

Close Reading 1: Read for Story Elements

"Fox and Crow" is mostly about a clever fox that tricks a trusting crow. Read the fable and underline the key elements of the story. Then complete the graphic organizer.

Collaborative Conversations

Beginning
Middle
End

Discuss your answers with a partner. When you speak, state how your ideas explain the key elements of the story. When you listen, ask questions to clarify what the speaker says.

Sentence Frames:

Speaker: The main problem of the story is . . .

At the end of the story . . .

Listener: Why did you choose this detail?

Why is this important to the story?

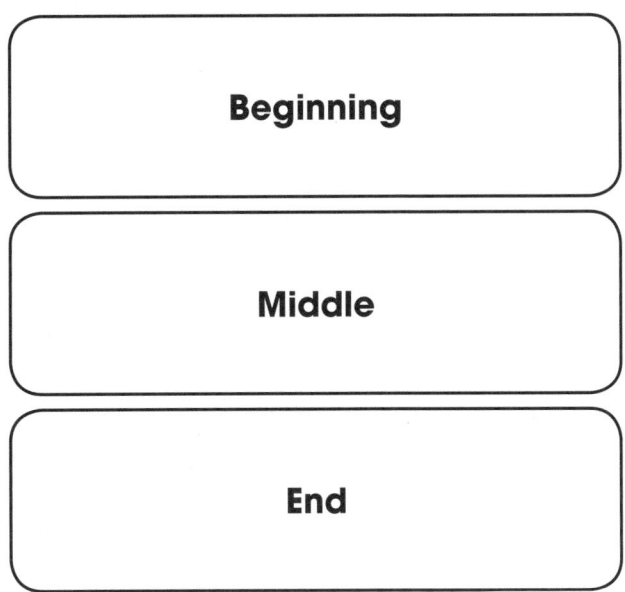

Name____ Date__________

Close Reading 2: Build Vocabulary

Reread the text. Locate each word or phrase, and identify context clues to determine its meaning. Underline the context clues as you read. Share your definitions or meanings with your partner and check your definitions, using a dictionary.

Word or Phrase	Context Clues	What the Text Says It Means
landed		
lovely		
glisten		
snagged		

Think-Share-Write

Collaborate with your partner to generate new sentences showing your understanding of each word or phrase. Choose two of the new sentences and write them in the space below.

____

____

____

____

Name____ Date__________

Close Reading 3: Identify Text Structure Examples

Part I: Read and Annotate

In this text, the author mainly uses a sequence text structure. Reread the text and underline examples of this text structure. Be sure to underline any signal words or phrases used by the author that reinforce the sequence text structure.

Part II: Collaborative Conversations

With a partner, discuss your examples using the following questions.

Discussion Questions	Our Notes
1. What text signal words helped you identify your examples?	
2. Did the author use signal words? How did you identify the order of events without signal words?	
3. How does a sequence text structure help you understand the main idea of this text?	

Part III: Visualize

Draw a picture of what the author describes in paragraphs 6 and 7. Share your drawing with a partner. How similar or different are your drawings?

Name_______________________ Date__________

Close Reading 4: Build Deeper Understanding

Collaborative Conversations

Reread the text with a partner and discuss the questions. Use information from the text and your ideas to answer the questions. In your discussion, remember to express your ideas clearly and ask questions to better understand each other.

Close Reading Questions	What is the author's purpose for writing this fable?	What lesson does Crow learn?	What do you think Crow will do the next time she sees Fox?
Text Evidence			
Inference/ Answer			

Name______________________________________ Date__________

Apply Knowledge Through Writing

Part I: Collaborative Conversations

With a partner, read and analyze the prompt. Use the following questions in your discussion.

Writing Prompt

In "Fox and Crow," the author tells about a clever fox that tricks a trusting crow. What should Crow have done when Fox asked her to sing? Write a short essay. Support your ideas with information from the story.

Analyze the Prompt Question	**My Thoughts**
Is this prompt opinion/argument or narrative?	
What is it asking me to write about?	
What are my ideas about this prompt?	

Part II: Write

Develop and write a short opinion essay. Be sure to:

1. introduce your topic and state your opinion,
2. use text evidence to support your reasons,
3. use linking words and phrases,
4. add a concluding sentence.

Name____ Date__________

Passage 6: Poem
The Land of Nod

by Robert Louis Stevenson

From breakfast on through all the day
At home among my friends I stay,
But every night I go abroad
Afar into the land of Nod.

All by myself I have to go,
With none to tell me what to do—
All alone beside the streams
And up the mountain-sides of dreams.

Name________________________________ Date________

The strangest things are there for me,
Both things to eat and things to see,
And many frightening sights abroad
Till morning in the land of Nod.

Try as I like to find the way,
I never can get back by day,
Nor can remember plain and clear
The curious music that I hear.

Name____ Date__________

Close Reading 1: Read for Poetry Elements

"The Land of Nod" describes journeys the author takes in his sleep. Read the poem and underline the words that describe the land of Nod. Think about how the author describes what happens when he dreams. Then complete the graphic organizer, using the details from the poem.

The author takes journeys in his sleep.

Collaborative Conversations

Discuss your answers with a partner. When you speak, state the details you underlined and explain why you think they help the reader imagine the land of Nod. When you listen, ask questions to clarify what the speaker says.

Sentence Frames:

Speaker: A key detail that supports the main idea is . . .

This detail helps me imagine . . .

Listener: Could you tell me more about that detail?

What evidence in the text leads you to say that?

Name____ Date__________

Close Reading 2: Build Vocabulary

Reread the text. Locate each word or phrase, and identify context clues to determine its meaning. Underline the context clues as you read. Share definitions or meanings with your partner and check your definitions, using a dictionary.

Word or Phrase	Context Clues	What the Text Says It Means
abroad		
land of Nod		
frightening		
way		
curious		

Think-Share-Write

Collaborate with your partner to generate new sentences showing your understanding of each word or phrase. Choose two of the new sentences and write them in the space below.

____

____

____

Name_______________________________________ Date__________

Close Reading 3: Identify Text Structure Examples

Part I: Read and Annotate

In this text, the author mainly uses a descriptive text structure. Reread the text and underline examples of this text structure. Be sure to underline any signal words or phrases that reinforce the text structure.

Part II: Collaborative Conversations

With a partner, discuss your examples using the following questions.

Discussion Questions	Our Notes
1. What text signal words helped you identify your examples?	
2. Did the author always use signal words?	
3. How does a descriptive text structure help you understand this text?	

Part III: Visualize

Draw a picture of what the author wants you to see while reading the poem. Share your drawing with a partner. How similar or different are your drawings?

Name____ Date__________

Close Reading 4: Build Deeper Understanding

Collaborative Conversations

Reread the text with a partner and discuss the questions. Use information from the text and your ideas to answer the questions. In your discussion, remember to express your ideas clearly and ask questions to better understand each other.

Close Reading Questions	What comparison does the author use to describe his dreams?	Does the author enjoy his trips to the land of Nod? How do you know?	What is the author's purpose for writing this poem?
Text Evidence			
Inference/ Answer			

Name________________________________ Date__________

Apply Knowledge Through Writing

Part I: Collaborative Conversations

With a partner, read and analyze the prompt. Use the following questions in your discussion.

Writing Prompt

The author of "The Land of Nod" writes about the journeys he takes in his dreams. Write a poem that describes where you go in your dreams. Use sensory details that describe what you see, feel, and hear. Your poem does not need to rhyme.

Analyze the Prompt Question	**My Thoughts**
Is this opinion/argument or narrative?	
What is it asking me to write about?	
What are my ideas about this prompt?	

Part II: Write

Develop and write a poem. Be sure to:

1. describe where you go in your dreams,
2. use a descriptive text structure,
3. use sensory details.

Name____ Date__________

Passage 7: Historical Fiction
The Dust Bowl

by Michelle Olmsted

1 *In the 1930s, dust storms destroyed farms in the southern Plains. Many families had to flee their homes. Read how Charlotte and her older brother, Henry, feel about leaving their Oklahoma farm.*

2 Dear Diary,

3 Tomorrow we leave for California. Daddy says life will be better there. We will not have to wear dust masks to walk to school. And we will be able to play outside again.

4 I don't remember what life was like before the storms. I was just three years old when the dust blew in. Now everything is covered in dirt. Somehow the dust even gets into our cupboards and fills our bowls.

5 But all I can think about is what I will miss here. Mamma says I can only take some clothes, one book, and my doll

continued

Name________________________________ Date__________

Millie. Everything else must stay behind. I will miss my books and games. But mostly I will miss my best friends, Elsa and Betty. I said good-bye to them today at school. I don't think I have ever cried so hard. I wonder if I will make new friends in California.

6 Charlotte

7 Dear Diary,

8 I can't sleep. We are moving to California tomorrow. Mamma and Daddy say it will be an adventure. I am nervous and excited.

9 I was born on this farm. It is my home. Before the dust storms, I thought I would grow up to be a farmer like Daddy. But crops don't grow on our land anymore. The soil is too dry. I know we must leave.

10 I will miss our farm, but I am excited to see California. Mamma says we may even live near the ocean. Imagine that! I don't even know how to swim!

11 Henry

Name______________________________ Date__________

Close Reading 1: Read for Story Elements

"The Dust Bowl" is mostly about a brother and sister who are about to leave their Oklahoma farm. Read the story and underline key details that tell how they feel about leaving. Then complete the graphic organizer using story details.

Collaborative Conversations

Discuss your answers with a partner. When you speak, state the details you underlined and explain why you think they tell about the characters. When you listen, ask questions to clarify what the speaker says.

How Charlotte Feels About Moving	How Henry Feels About Moving

Sentence Frames:

Speaker: The character feels . . .

I know this because . . .

Listener: Can you tell me more about this idea?

What evidence in the text leads you to say that?

Name____ Date__________

Close Reading 2: Build Vocabulary

Reread the text. Locate each word or phrase, and identify context clues to determine its meaning. Underline the context clues as you read. Share definitions or meanings with your partner and check your definitions, using a dictionary.

Word or Phrase	Context Clues	What the Text Says It Means
southern Plains		
flee		
dust masks		
adventure		
soil		

Think-Share-Write

Collaborate with your partner to generate new sentences showing your understanding of each word or phrase. Choose two of the new sentences and write them in the space below.

____

____

____

Name____ Date__________

Close Reading 3: Identify Text Structure Examples

Part I: Read and Annotate

Reread the text and underline examples of the descriptive text structure. Underline any signal words or phrases used by the author that reinforce the descriptive text structure.

Part II: Collaborative Conversations

With a partner, discuss your examples using the following questions.

Discussion Questions	Our Notes
1. What text signal words helped you identify your examples?	
2. Did the author use signal words? Explain how you identified a relationship without signal words.	
3. How does a descriptive text structure help you understand the main idea?	

Part III: Visualize

Draw a picture of what the author describes in paragraph 3. Share your drawing with a partner. How similar or different are your drawings?

Name____ Date__________

Close Reading 4: Build Deeper Understanding

Collaborative Conversations

Reread the text with a partner and discuss the questions. Use information from the text and your ideas to answer the questions. In your discussion, remember to express your ideas clearly and ask questions to better understand each other.

Close Reading Questions	What is Charlotte's point of view about moving?	What is Henry's point of view about moving?	What is the author's purpose for writing this text?
Text Evidence			
Inference/ Answer			

Name____ Date__________

Apply Knowledge Through Writing

Part I: Collaborative Conversations

With a partner, read and analyze the prompt. Use the following questions in your discussion.

Writing Prompt

In "The Dust Bowl," Charlotte and Henry describe their thoughts and feelings the night before they leave. Write a short essay that tells how they are alike and how they are different. Support your ideas with information from the text.

Analyze the Prompt Question	My Thoughts
Is this prompt narrative or informative/explanatory?	
What is it asking me to write about?	
What are my ideas about it?	

Part II: Write

Develop and write a short informative essay. Be sure to:

1. state your topic,
2. use details and text evidence to develop your topic,
3. use linking words and phrases,
4. add a concluding sentence.

Name____ Date__________

Passage 8: Technical Text
How to Grow a Pineapple Plant

by Michelle Olmsted

1 Did you know you can grow your own pineapple plant at home?

2 Follow these simple steps to grow a pineapple plant. You begin with the top of a ripe pineapple.

Things You Need

ripe, juicy pineapple

knife

gravel

soil

large clay pot with a drainage hole at the bottom

Directions

3 Cut off the leafy crown from the top of a ripe pineapple.

4 Place the crown in a dry, dark place for several days.

Name____ Date__________

5 Twist off the base, the section below the leaves, to remove all of the sweet fruit flesh.

6 Pull off the small bottom leaves.

7 Pour a layer of gravel into the bottom of a clay pot.

8 Fill the rest of the pot with soil.

9 Make a small hole in the soil.

10 Plant the pineapple crown in the center of the pot.

11 Be sure that the pineapple is straight and firmly planted in the soil.

12 Water the soil and leaves once a week; allow extra water to flow out.

13 Watch your plant grow!

14 A new pineapple plant can take up to two years to bear fruit. If you live in a warm climate, you can keep the potted plant outside. Bring the plant indoors if the temperature drops below freezing.

Name____ Date__________

Close Reading 1: Read for Main Ideas and Details

"How to Grow a Pineapple Plant" teaches how to grow a pineapple plant at home. Read the text and underline the key details that support the main idea. Then complete the graphic organizer using details from the text.

How to Grow a Pineapple Plant

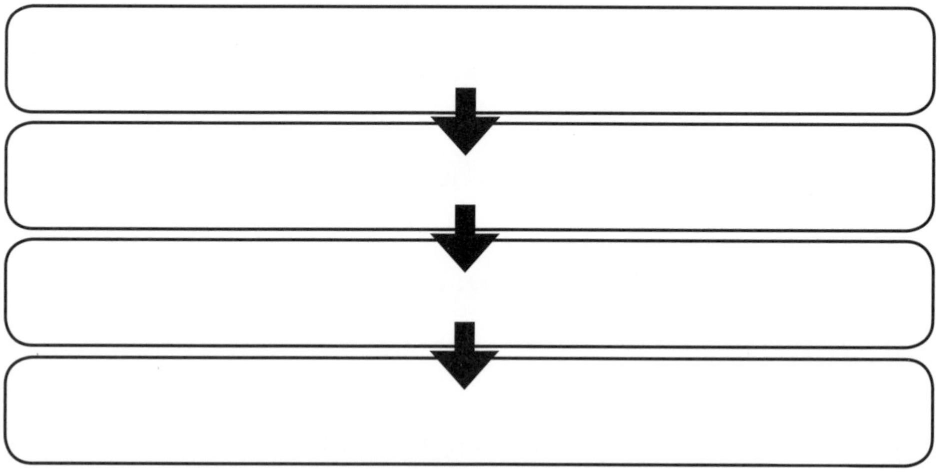

Collaborative Conversations

Discuss your flowchart with a partner. When you speak, state your ideas and explain why you think they are key steps to growing a pineapple plant. When you listen, ask questions to clarify what the speaker says.

Sentence Frames:

Speaker: A key step is . . .

I know this because . . .

Listener: Why did you choose this step?

Could you tell me more about this idea?

Name______________________________ Date________

Close Reading 2: Build Vocabulary

Reread the text. Locate each word or phrase, and identify context clues to determine its meaning. Underline the context clues as you read. Share your definitions or meanings with your partner and check your definitions, using a dictionary.

Word or Phrase	Context Clues	What the Text Says It Means
ripe		
drainage		
crown		
base		
flesh		
bear		

Think-Share-Write

Collaborate with your partner to generate new sentences showing your understanding of each word or phrase. Choose two of the new sentences and write them in the space below.

____

____

____

____

Name____ Date__________

Close Reading 3: Identify Text Structure Examples

Part I: Read and Annotate

In this text, the author mainly uses a sequence text structure. Reread the text and underline examples of this text structure. Be sure to underline any signal words or phrases used by the author that reinforce the sequence text structure.

Part II: Collaborative Conversations

With a partner, discuss your examples, using the following questions.

Discussion Questions	Our Notes
1. What text signal words helped you identify your examples?	
2. Did the author always use signal words? Explain how you were able to identify a sequence without them.	
3. How does a sequence text structure help you understand the main idea of this text?	

Part III: Visualize

Draw a picture of what the author describes in 10–13. Share your drawing with a partner. How similar or different are your drawings?

Name________________________________ Date__________

Close Reading 4: Build Deeper Understanding

Collaborative Conversations

Reread the text with a partner and discuss the questions. Use information from the text and your ideas to answer the questions. In your discussion, remember to express your ideas clearly and ask questions to better understand each other.

Close Reading Questions	What is the author's purpose?	What is the author's point of view about growing a pineapple plant at home?	Where should you keep your pineapple plant if you live in a cold climate?
Text Evidence			
Inference/ Answer			

Name______________________________ Date________

Apply Knowledge Through Writing

Part I: Collaborative Conversations

With a partner, read and analyze the prompt. Use the following questions in your discussion.

Writing Prompt

In "How to Grow a Pineapple Plant," the author explains how to grow a pineapple plant at home. Imagine that you followed these steps at home. Write a short story about your experience. Support your writing with evidence from the text.

Analyze the Prompt Question	My Thoughts
Is this prompt narrative or opinion/argument?	
What is it asking me to write about?	
What are my ideas about this prompt?	

Part II: Write

Develop and write a short narrative. Be sure to:

1. develop the characters through actions and events,
2. use signal words showing time,
3. add an ending.

Name______________________________ Date________

Passage 9: Personal Narrative
Boris

by the Central Intelligence Agency

1 *Dogs communicate in many ways. Some, like Boris, even have important jobs to do. If Boris could write, he might want to tell you about his work.*

2 Hi there! My name is Boris. I'm a Yellow Lab. I was born on February 15, and I weigh 67 pounds. I was brought up in a program called "Puppies Behind Bars." My trainers there taught me how to sit and stay.

3 On the weekends, I stayed with families that volunteered to look after me. I was with a new family each weekend. It got me used to people and children. I love being around people. I especially like to play with kids who grab my tail.

4 When I was one, I learned how to smell for explosive odors. I loved the training because I learned that when I found an explosive odor, I would get food. I love to eat!

continued

Name____ Date_________

5 During the training, I met my partner, Officer Eric. We formed a wonderful friendship. Officer Eric and I learned how to work together; we are an excellent team. Officer Eric and I now work together at the CIA.

6 One of my favorite things to do is to jump into a lake. At first, I was scared to swim. But then Officer Eric threw my favorite toy far out into the water. It would have drifted away if I didn't jump in after it. I'm fearless now, and I sometimes scare Officer Eric when I swim far out in the water. I am a retriever, after all!

7 I am lucky to have a cool job and a great partner who loves me. I love to play fetch with anyone who wants to play. Sometimes, I pretend that I am a tough dog. I will play bite and wrestle with Officer Eric and his friends, but I would never actually bite or hurt anybody.

Name____________________________________ Date__________

Close Reading 1: Read for Main Ideas and Details

"Boris" is about a dog that works at the CIA. Read the text and underline the key details that support the main idea. Complete the graphic organizer using details from the text.

Collaborative Conversations

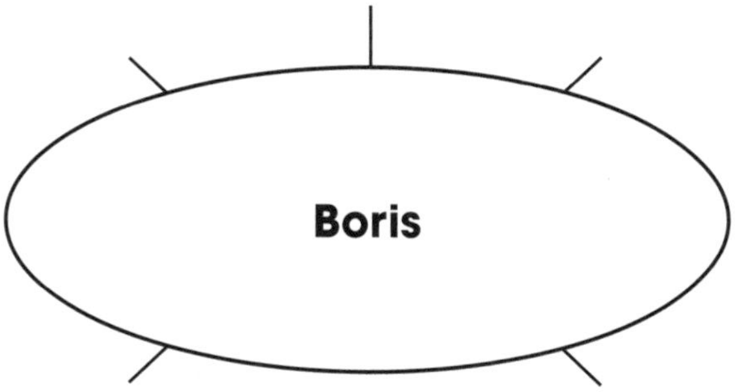

Discuss your answers with a partner. When you speak, state your ideas and explain why you think they tell key details about Boris. When you listen, ask questions to clarify what the speaker says.

Sentence Frames:

Speaker: Based on the information in the text . . .

The text focuses on . . .

Listener: Why did you choose this detail?

Could you tell me more about this idea?

Name____ Date__________

Close Reading 2: Build Vocabulary

Reread the text. Locate each word or phrase, and identify context clues to determine its meaning. Underline the context clues as you read. Share your definitions or meanings with your partner and check definitions using a dictionary.

Word or Phrase	**Context Clues**	**What the Text Says It Means**
trainers		
volunteered		
odors		
retriever		

Think-Share-Write

Collaborate with your partner to generate new sentences that show your understanding of each word or phrase. Choose two of the new sentences and write them in the space below.

____

____

____

Name______________________________ Date________

Close Reading 3: Identify Text Structure Examples

Part I: Read and Annotate

In this text, the author mainly uses a descriptive text structure. Reread the text and underline examples of this text structure. Be sure to underline any signal words or phrases used by the author that reinforce the descriptive text structure.

Part II: Collaborative Conversations

With a partner, discuss examples using the following questions.

Discussion Questions	Our Notes
1. What text signal words helped you identify your examples?	
2. Did the author always use signal words? Explain how you identified a relationship without signal words.	
3. How does a descriptive text structure help you understand the main idea?	

Part III: Visualize

Draw a picture of what the author describes in paragraphs 5 and 6. Share your drawing with a partner. How similar or different are your drawings?

Name_______________________________________ Date__________

Close Reading 4: Build Deeper Understanding

Collaborative Conversations

Reread the text with a partner and discuss the questions. Use information from the text and your ideas to answer the questions. In your discussion, remember to express your ideas clearly and ask questions to better understand each other.

Close Reading Questions	What is the author's purpose for writing this text?	What is the author's point of view about working at the CIA?	What words does the author use to describe Boris? What does this tell you about the author?
Text Evidence			
Inference/ Answer			

Name____ Date__________

Apply Knowledge Through Writing

Part I: Collaborative Conversations

With a partner, read and analyze the prompt. Use the following questions in your discussion.

Writing Prompt

In "Boris," the author tells about a dog that works at the CIA. The text is written from the dog's point of view. Write a short essay that tells about Boris and his job. Support your ideas with information from the text.

Analyze the Prompt Question	**My Thoughts**
Is this prompt narrative or informative/explanatory?	
What is it asking me to write about?	
What are my ideas about it?	

Part II: Write

Develop and write a short informative essay. Be sure to:

1. state your topic,
2. use details and text evidence to develop your topic,
3. use linking words and phrases,
4. add a concluding sentence.

Name______________________________ Date________

Passage 10: Science Article
How Do Clouds Form?

by David Hitt

1 We can see clouds on many days when we look up in the sky. They come in many shapes and sizes. Sometimes they even look like animals or objects around us. But how do clouds form?

2 A cloud is made of water drops or ice crystals floating in the sky. The sky can be full of water. But most of the time you can't see the water. The drops of water are too small to see. They have turned into a gas called water vapor. As the water vapor goes higher in the sky, the air gets cooler. The cooler air causes the water droplets to start to stick to things like bits of dust, ice, or sea salt.

3 Sometimes those droplets join with other droplets. Then they turn into larger drops. When that happens, gravity causes them to fall to Earth. We call the falling water drops rain. When the air is colder, the water may

Name______________________ Date________

form snowflakes instead. Freezing rain, sleet, or even hail can fall from clouds.

4 There are many kinds of clouds. Clouds get their names in two ways. One way is to name them based on where they are found in the sky. Some clouds are high up in the sky. Other clouds form closer to Earth's surface. In fact, low clouds can even touch the ground. These clouds are called fog. Middle clouds are found between low and high clouds.

5 Another way clouds are named is by using their shape. Cirrus clouds are high clouds. They look like feathers. Cumulus clouds are middle clouds. These clouds look like giant cotton balls in the sky. Stratus clouds are low clouds. They cover the sky like bedsheets.

6 So the next time you look up in the sky, think about how clouds form and the role they play in Earth's weather.

Name________________________________ Date__________

Close Reading 1: Read for Main Ideas and Details

"How Do Clouds Form?" is mostly about how clouds form and the role they play in Earth's weather. Read the article and underline key supporting details. Then complete the graphic organizer using details from the article.

Cause **Effect**

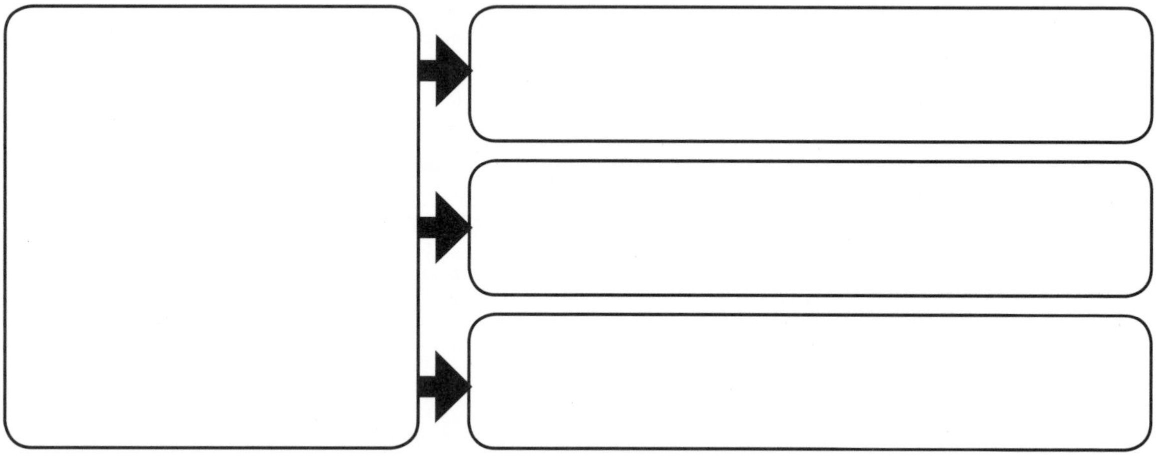

Collaborative Conversations

Discuss your answers with a partner. When you speak, state the key details you underlined and explain how these details support the main idea. When you listen, ask questions to clarify what the speaker says.

Sentence Frames:

Speaker: A key idea that supports the main idea is . . .

I know this because . . .

Listener: Why did you choose this detail?

Could you tell me more about this idea?

Name____ Date__________

Close Reading 2: Build Vocabulary

Reread the text. Locate each word or phrase, and identify context clues to determine its meaning. Underline the context clues as you read. Share definitions or meanings with your partner and check definitions in a dictionary.

Word or Phrase	Context Clues	What the Text Says It Means
water vapor		
droplets		
gravity		
surface		
fog		

Think-Share-Write

Collaborate with your partner to generate new sentences that show your understanding of each word or phrase. Choose two of the new sentences and write them in the space below.

____

____

____

Name____ Date__________

Close Reading 3: Identify Text Structure Examples

Part I: Read and Annotate

In this text, the author mainly uses a cause-and-effect text structure. Reread the text and underline examples of this text structure. Be sure to underline any signal words or phrases that reinforce the cause-and-effect text structure.

Part II: Collaborative Conversations

With a partner, discuss your examples using these questions.

Discussion Questions	Our Notes
1. What text signal words helped you identify your examples?	
2. Did the author always use signal words? Explain how you identified a relationship without signal words.	
3. How does a cause-and-effect text structure help you understand the main idea of this text?	

Part III: Visualize

Draw a picture of what the author describes in paragraph 5. Share your drawing with a partner. How similar or different are your drawings?

Name____ Date_________

Close Reading 4: Build Deeper Understanding

Collaborative Conversations

Reread the text with a partner and discuss the questions. Use information from the text and your ideas to answer the questions. In your discussion, remember to express your ideas clearly and ask questions to better understand each other.

Close Reading Questions	What is the author's purpose for writing this science article?	Why does the author say that clouds sometimes look like animals or objects?	How do clouds affect our weather?
Text Evidence			
Inference/ Answer			

Name________________________________ Date__________

Apply Knowledge Through Writing

Part I: Collaborative Conversations

With a partner, read and analyze the prompt. Use the following questions in your discussion.

Writing Prompt

In "How Do Clouds Form?" the author tells about clouds and the role clouds play in Earth's weather. Write a short essay that tells how Earth and its weather would be different if there were no clouds. Support your idea with text evidence.

Analyze the Prompt Question	My Thoughts
Is this prompt opinion/ argument or informative/ explanatory?	
What is it asking me to write about?	
What are my ideas about this prompt?	

Part II: Write

Develop and write a short informative essay. Be sure to:

1. state your topic,
2. use details and text evidence to develop your topic,
3. use linking words and phrases,
4. add a concluding sentence.

Name________________________________ Date________

Passage 11: Social Studies Article

Communities

by Michelle Olmsted

1 Do you live in the city or in the country? Or maybe you live somewhere in between. The place where you live and go to school is called a community.

City

2 People who live in a city live in an urban community. A city has many tall buildings. These buildings are close together. Many people live in apartments rather than houses. There is not a lot of open land in a city, so children play in community parks.

3 Urban communities are crowded with people, so schools are usually large. School buildings may be three or more stories tall. Many students take public transportation, like a bus or subway, to get to school. Many students walk, too.

Town

4 A suburban community is located in a town outside of a city. A suburb

continued

Name________________________ Date__________

has neighborhoods where people live in houses or apartments. There is more open land in a suburb than in a city. Many houses have yards. There are also community parks.

5 Many schools in suburban communities have playgrounds and sports fields. Students may ride in a school bus or in a car to get to school. They may walk, too.

Country

6 Some people live in the country, or a rural community. The country is where farms are located. Farmers grow crops or raise animals in rural communities. There is a lot of open land. There are few homes and buildings.

7 There are fewer people in rural communities, so schools are usually small. Rural schools may have only one classroom. Since homes and buildings are far apart, most children go to school in a school bus or a car.

8 What kind of community do you live in?

Name____ Date__________

Close Reading 1: Read for Main Ideas and Details

"Communities" is mostly about three types of communities, or places where people live. Read the article and underline the key details that tell about each type. Then complete the graphic organizer using details from the article.

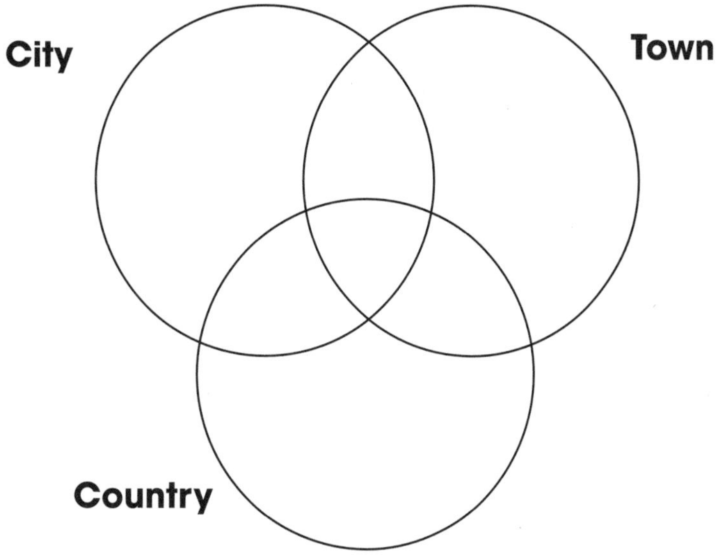

Collaborative Conversations

Discuss your answers with a partner. When you speak, state why these are key details about the three types of communities. When you listen, ask questions to clarify what the speaker says.

Sentence Frames:

Speaker: Based on the information in the text . . .

I know this because . . .

Listener: Why did you choose this detail?

Could you tell me more about this idea?

Name________________________________ Date__________

Close Reading 2: Build Vocabulary

Reread the text. Locate each word or phrase, and identify context clues to determine its meaning. Underline the context clues as you read. Share definitions or meanings with your partner and check them using a dictionary.

Word or Phrase	Context Clues	What the Text Says It Means
community		
urban community		
public transportation		
suburban community		
neighborhoods		

Think-Share-Write

Collaborate with your partner to generate new sentences showing your understanding of each word or phrase. Choose two of the new sentences and write them in the space below.

____

____

____

Name______________________________ Date________

Close Reading 3: Identify Text Structure Examples

Part I: Read and Annotate

In this text, the author uses a compare-and-contrast text structure. Reread the text and underline examples of this text structure. Underline any signal words or phrases that reinforce the compare-and-contrast text structure.

Part II: Collaborative Conversations

With a partner, discuss examples using the questions.

Discussion Questions	Our Notes
1. What text signal words helped you identify your examples?	
2. Did the author always use signal words? Explain how you identified a compare-and-contrast relationship without them.	
3. How does a compare-and-contrast text structure help you understand the main idea of this text?	

Part III: Visualize

Draw a picture of what the author describes in paragraphs 3, 5, and 7. Share your drawing with a partner. How similar or different are your drawings?

Name______________________________ Date__________

Close Reading 4: Build Deeper Understanding

Collaborative Conversations

Reread the text with a partner and discuss the questions. Use information from the text and your ideas to answer the questions. In your discussion, remember to express your ideas clearly and ask questions to better understand each other.

Close Reading Questions	How are schools in each community similar? How are they different?	What is the author's purpose for writing this article?	What kind of community do you live in? How do you know?
Text Evidence			
Inference/ Answer			

Name____ Date__________

Apply Knowledge Through Writing

Part I: Collaborative Conversations

With a partner, read and analyze the prompt. Use the following questions in your discussion.

Writing Prompt

In "Communities," the author tells about three different types of communities. Write a short essay that tells about your community. Tell whether you live in an urban, suburban, or rural community. Support your writing with text evidence.

Analyze the Prompt Question	My Thoughts
Is this prompt informative/ explanatory or opinion/ argument?	
What is it asking me to write about?	
What are my ideas about it?	

Part II: Write

Develop and write a short informative essay. Be sure to:

1. state your topic,
2. use details and text evidence to develop your topic,
3. use linking words and phrases,
4. add a concluding sentence.

Name____ Date________

Passage 12: Science Article
What Is Rabies?

by the Centers for Disease Control and Prevention

1 Rabies is a disease that affects the brain. It's usually passed from animal to animal. It can also be passed from animals to people. It's caused by a virus. A virus is a very tiny germ. You can see that germ only if you have a special microscope.

2 Any mammal can get rabies. Do you remember what a mammal is? Mammals are warm-blooded animals with fur. We're mammals. So are most of our pets, like cats and dogs. Cows and horses are mammals. So are wild animals, like foxes and skunks. We can all get rabies. Even bats can get rabies!

3 How do you know if an animal has rabies?

4 You can't tell if an animal has rabies by just looking at it. A clue is if the animal is acting strangely. Some animals may act mad when they have rabies. They will be hostile and may try

Name_______________________________________ Date_________

to bite. Some animals with rabies look as if they are foaming at the mouth. Rabies makes them have more saliva and that makes them drool.

5 Other animals may act timid or shy when they have rabies. This is the most common kind. A wild animal might move slowly or act tame. You might be able to easily get close to it. Since that's not the way wild animals usually act, you should remember that something could be wrong.

6 The only way doctors can know for sure if an animal has rabies is to do a laboratory test. It is safest to never feed or approach a wild animal. Be careful of pets that you don't know. If you see a stray dog or cat, don't pet it. If any animal is acting strangely, ask a trusted adult to call your local animal control officer for help.

Name____ Date________

Close Reading 1: Read for Main Ideas and Details

"What Is Rabies?" is mostly about the signs and symptoms of rabies. Read the article and underline the key details that support the main idea. Then complete the graphic organizer, using details from the article.

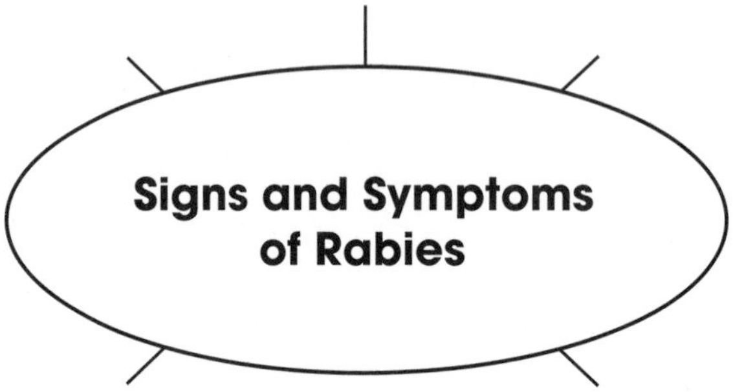

Collaborative Conversations

Discuss your answers with a partner. When you speak, state the details you underlined and explain why you think they tell about the signs and symptoms of rabies. When you listen, ask questions to clarify what the speaker says.

Sentence Frames:

Speaker: The author's main point is . . .

Based on the information in the text . . .

Listener: What evidence in the text leads you to say that?

What details does the author use to describe that?

Name________________________________ Date________

Close Reading 2: Build Vocabulary

Reread the text. Locate each word or phrase, and identify context clues to determine its meaning. Underline the context clues as you read. Share definitions or meanings with your partner and check them using a dictionary.

Word or Phrase	Context Clues	What the Text Says It Means
rabies		
mammal		
hostile		
timid		
stray		

Think-Share-Write

Collaborate with your partner to generate new sentences showing your understanding of each word or phrase. Choose two of the new sentences and write them in the space below.

____

____

____

____

Name________________________________ Date__________

Close Reading 3: Identify Text Structure Examples

Part I: Read and Annotate

In this text, the author mainly uses a descriptive text structure. Reread the text and underline examples of this text structure. Be sure to underline any signal words or phrases that reinforce the descriptive text structure.

Part II: Collaborative Conversations

With a partner, discuss examples using the questions.

Discussion Questions	Our Notes
1. What text signal words helped you identify your examples?	
2. Did the author always use signal words? Explain how you identified a relationship without signal words.	
3. How does a descriptive text structure help you understand the main idea of this text?	

Part III: Visualize

Draw a picture of what the author describes in paragraphs 3 and 4. Share your drawing with a partner. How similar or different are your drawings?

Name____ Date__________

Close Reading 4: Build Deeper Understanding

Collaborative Conversations

Reread the text with a partner and discuss the questions. Use information from the text and your ideas to answer the questions. In your discussion, remember to express your ideas clearly and ask questions to better understand each other.

Close Reading Questions	What is the author's purpose for writing this article?	What is the author's point of view about going near wild or stray animals?	What should you do if you notice your pet acting strangely or foaming at the mouth?
Text Evidence			
Inference/ Answer			

Name____ Date__________

Apply Knowledge Through Writing

Part I: Collaborative Conversations

With a partner, read and analyze the prompt. Use the following questions in your discussion.

Writing Prompt

In "What Is Rabies?" the author writes about the signs and symptoms of rabies. Write a short story about a character who sees an animal that may have rabies. Describe the animal and the character's response. Support your ideas with information from the story.

Analyze the Prompt Question	My Thoughts
Is this prompt narrative or informative/ explanatory?	
What is it asking me to write about?	
What are my ideas about this prompt?	

Part II: Write

Develop and write a short narrative. Be sure to:

1. develop the characters through actions and events,
2. use signal words showing time,
3. add an ending.

Name________________________________ Date________

Passage 13: Biography
Harriet Tubman

by America's Library

1 When Harriet Tubman was born, her name was Araminta Ross. She and her brothers and sisters were born into slavery. As a child, Araminta was sent by her master to a family to be a babysitter. She had to stay awake all night so that the baby wouldn't cry. If Araminta fell asleep, the baby's mother whipped her. From this young age, she was determined to become free.

2 Araminta later married a free black man named John Tubman and took his last name. She also changed her first name, taking her mother's name, Harriet. Years later she worried that she and the other slaves on the plantation were going to be sold. Harriet decided to run away.

3 Harriet's husband refused to go with her. She set out with her two brothers instead. Northern states did not allow slavery. She followed the North Star in the sky to guide her there. Her brothers

continued

Name____ Date__________

became frightened and turned back. Harriet continued on and reached the North. She found work as a servant. Here she saved her money so she could return and help others.

4 Harriet returned to the slave states many times to help others escape. It was dangerous to be a runaway slave. There were rewards for their capture. Whenever Harriet led a group of slaves to freedom, she placed herself in great danger. She was breaking the law by helping slaves escape. There was a large reward offered for her capture.

5 Harriet made 19 trips and helped bring 300 people to freedom. She rescued slaves by using the Underground Railroad—many different secret routes to freedom and the brave guides called "conductors" who led the slaves to safety. During these dangerous trips she helped rescue members of her own family, including her parents. She was never captured and never failed to deliver her "passengers" to safety.

Name______________________________ Date________

Close Reading 1: Read for Main Ideas and Details

"Harriet Tubman" is mostly about an enslaved woman who risked her life to escape and to help others to escape slavery. Read the biography and underline key details that support the main idea. Then complete the graphic organizer, using text details.

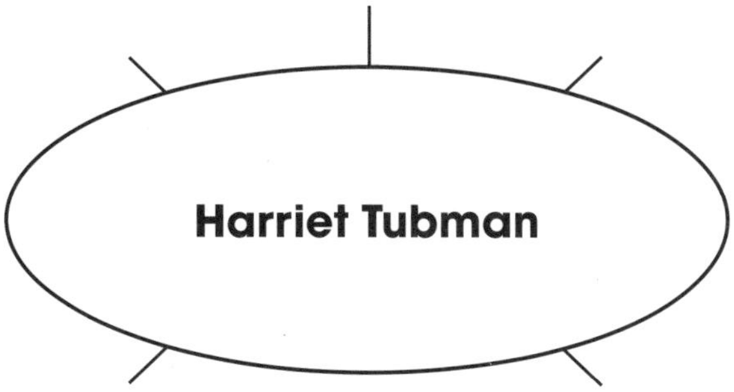

Collaborative Conversations

Discuss your answers with a partner. When you speak, state what the details you underlined tell about Harriet Tubman and how she helped bring slaves to freedom. When you listen, ask questions to clarify what the speaker says.

Sentence Frames:

Speaker: A key idea that supports the main idea is . . .

I know this because . . .

Listener: Could you tell me more about this idea?

How does that detail support the main idea?

Name______________________________ Date__________

Close Reading 2: Build Vocabulary

Reread the text. Locate each word or phrase, and identify context clues to determine its meaning. Underline the context clues as you read. Share definitions or meanings with your partner and check definitions in a dictionary.

Word or Phrase	**Context Clues**	**What the Text Says It Means**
slavery		
plantation		
refused		
runaway slave		
capture		

Think-Share-Write

Collaborate with your partner to generate new sentences that show your understanding of each word or phrase. Choose two of the new sentences and write them in the space below.

____

____

____

Name______________________________ Date__________

Close Reading 3: Identify Text Structure Examples

Part I: Read and Annotate

In this text, the author mainly uses a sequence text structure. Reread the text and underline examples of this text structure. Be sure to underline any signal words or phrases that reinforce the sequence text structure.

Part II: Collaborative Conversations

With a partner, discuss your examples using the following questions.

Discussion Questions	Our Notes
1. What signal words helped you identify your examples?	
2. Did the author always use signal words? Explain how you identified a sequence without signal words.	
3. How does a sequence text structure help you understand the main idea of this text?	

Part III: Visualize

Draw a picture of what the author describes in paragraphs 4 and 5. Share your drawing with a partner. How similar or different are your drawings?

Name____ Date__________

Close Reading 4: Build Deeper Understanding

Collaborative Conversations

Reread the text with a partner and discuss the questions. Use information from the text and your ideas to answer the questions. In your discussion, remember to express your ideas clearly and ask questions to better understand each other.

Close Reading Questions	What is the author's purpose for writing this biography?	Based on the information in the text, how would you describe Harriet Tubman's character?	What is the author's point of view about Harriet Tubman's rescue missions?
Text Evidence		"	
Inference/ Answer			

Name_______________________________________ Date_________

Apply Knowledge Through Writing

Part I: Collaborative Conversations

With a partner, read and analyze the prompt. Use the following questions in your discussion.

Writing Prompt

In "Harriet Tubman," the author tells about a slave who risks her life to become free and to help others become free. Write a short story that describes Harriet Tubman's escape to the North. Support your ideas with information from the text.

Analyze the Prompt Question	My Thoughts
Is this prompt narrative or opinion/ argument?	
What is it asking me to write about?	
What are my ideas about this prompt?	

Part II: Write

Develop and write a short narrative. Be sure to:

1. develop the characters through actions and events,
2. use signal words showing time,
3. add an ending.

Name________________________________ Date__________

Passage 14: Newspaper Article
Playground Project

by Michelle Olmsted

1 The playground at Central Elementary is getting a new look. Students will soon enjoy a clean play area and a new vegetable garden. The project begins this weekend.

2 The cleanup will take place this Saturday from 8 a.m. to 2 p.m. Students and their families are encouraged to help. Helpers will pick up trash and paint the playground equipment.

3 Principal Baker hopes to have many helpers on Saturday. "It is a big job," she said. "Everyone should lend a hand." She also said that helpers should wear old clothes and shoes.

4 The cleanup is just the first step. After that, work will begin on a new garden. The garden will be located at the far end of the playground.

Name______________________________ Date________

5 Great Gardens donated all of the tools and materials. Experts from Great Gardens will build the garden beds. Then teachers and students will plant the vegetables.

6 “We are very excited about the new school garden,” Principal Baker said. “Every student will help care for the garden.”

7 “This project will teach students how to grow vegetables. They also learn how to prepare meals with them,” Principal Baker said.

8 Central Elementary will be the first school in Rockland to have a vegetable garden. Principal Baker hopes more schools in the area plant gardens, too.

Name____ Date__________

Close Reading 1: Read for Main Ideas and Details

"Playground Project" is a story about a school's playground cleanup and garden project. Read the newspaper article and underline the key details that support the main idea. Then complete the graphic organizer using details from the article.

Central Elementary's Playground Cleanup and Garden Project

Collaborative Conversations

Discuss your answers with a partner. When you speak, state the details you underlined and what they tell about the playground project. When you listen, ask questions to clarify what the speaker says.

Sentence Frames:

Speaker: The article focuses on . . .

Based on the information in the text . . .

Listener: Why did you choose this detail?

Why did you put the details in this order?

Name____ Date__________

Close Reading 2: Build Vocabulary

Reread the text. Locate each word or phrase, and identify context clues to determine its meaning. Underline the context clues as you read. Share definitions or meanings with your partner and check them in a dictionary.

Word or Phrase	Context Clues	What the Text Says It Means
project		
encouraged		
lend a hand		
donated		
experts		
prepare		

Think-Share-Write

Collaborate with your partner to generate new sentences showing your understanding of each word or phrase. Choose two of the new sentences and write them in the space below.

____

____

____

____

Name____ Date__________

Close Reading 3: Identify Text Structure Examples

Part I: Read and Annotate

In this text, the author mainly uses a sequence text structure. Reread the text and underline examples of this text structure. Be sure to underline any signal words or phrases that reinforce the sequence text structure.

Part II: Collaborative Conversations

With a partner, discuss examples using the questions.

Discussion Questions	Our Notes
1. What text signal words helped you identify your examples?	
2. Did the author always use signal words? Explain how you identified the order of events without signal words.	
3. How does a sequence text structure help you understand the main idea of this text?	

Part III: Visualize

Draw a picture of what the author wants you to see in paragraphs 4 and 5. Share your drawing with a partner. How similar or different are your drawings?

Name______________________________________ Date__________

Close Reading 4: Build Deeper Understanding

Collaborative Conversations

Reread the text with a partner and discuss the questions. Use information from the text and your ideas to answer the questions. In your discussion, remember to express your ideas clearly and ask questions to better understand each other.

Close Reading Questions	What is the author's purpose for writing this article?	What is the author's point of view about the project?	How will the success or failure of Central Elementary's garden affect other schools in the area?
Text Evidence			
Inference/ Answer			

Name______________________________ Date__________

Apply Knowledge Through Writing

Part I: Collaborative Conversations

With a partner, read and analyze the prompt. Use the following questions in your discussion.

Writing Prompt

In "Playground Project," the author tells about a school's playground cleanup and garden project. Write a short essay that tells what you think about the playground project. Support your viewpoint with details from the article.

Analyze the Prompt Question	**My Thoughts**
Is this prompt opinion/argument or narrative?	
What is it asking me to write about?	
What are my ideas about it?	

Part II: Write

Develop and write a short opinion essay. Be sure to:

1. introduce your topic and state your opinion,
2. give reasons for your opinion based on text evidence,
3. use linking words and phrases,
4. add a concluding sentence.

Sentence Frames

Speaker: A key idea that supports the main idea is . . .

I know this because . . .

Listener: Why did you choose this detail?

What evidence in the text leads you to say that?

Speaker: The main characters are . . .

The main problem in the story is . . .

Listener: What details does the author use to describe this?

What can you tell from that?

Speaker: This detail is important because . . .

Based on the information in the text . . .

Listener: Could you tell me more about that detail?

What details does the author use to describe that?

Speaker: The speaker's main point is . . .

Based on the information in the speech . . .

Listener: What information in the speech leads you to say that?

What details does the speaker use to describe that?

Speaker: This detail makes me think . . .

The author explores the idea that . . .

Listener: Why did you choose this detail?

Why did the author include this detail?

Rubrics

Narrative Writing Checklist

	Yes	No	Not Sure
1. My narrative has a strong lead that catches the reader's attention.			
2. I include specific details to establish the time, place, and characters involved.			
3. I use dialogue to develop experiences and events and to show the responses of characters to situations.			
4. I include description to help my readers visualize the events and characters.			
5. I include dialogue or express what people said.			
6. My narrative is logically sequenced.			
7. I use sequence (transitional) words and phrases to manage the sequence of events.			
8. My narrative has a strong ending.			
9. I tell my personal narrative using kid-friendly language.			
10. I use describing words, including adjectives and adverbs, to tell my story.			
11. I use both concrete and sensory language to convey experiences and events precisely.			
12. I provide a conclusion that follows from the experiences and events in my narrative.			

Quality Writing Checklist

I looked for and corrected . . .	Yes	No	Not Sure
sentence fragments and run-ons.			
parts of speech (pronouns, auxiliaries, adjectives, prepositions).			
grammar.			
indented paragraphs.			
punctuation.			
capitalization.			
spelling.			

Rubrics

Informative/Explanatory Writing Checklist

	Yes	No	Not Sure
1. I researched my topic and organized my information into notes that helped me write my text.			
2. I introduce my topic clearly and use words that grab my readers' attention.			
3. I keep my paper organized by grouping information together in a way that makes sense. I use paragraphs and sections.			
4. I use headings to organize my sections.			
5. The information in my report is accurate.			
6. I support my points with facts, definitions, concrete details, and quotations.			
7. I include graphics to support my information.			
8. I include captions that explain each graphic.			
9. I use linking words, signal words, and phrases to link ideas.			
10. My report includes different viewpoints so that I do not sway my readers to think one way.			
11. I include a strong conclusion that keeps my readers thinking.			
12. I choose words that make my text interesting to read and easy to understand. I include words that connect to the topic.			
13. I use at least one primary source.			
14. I use a formal voice.			

Quality Writing Checklist

I looked for and corrected . . .	Yes	No	Not Sure
sentence fragments and run-ons.			
parts of speech (pronouns, auxiliaries, adjectives, prepositions).			
grammar.			
indented paragraphs.			
punctuation.			
capitalization.			
spelling.			

Rubrics

Opinion/Argument Writing Checklist

	Yes	No	Not Sure
1. I introduce my topic with a lead that grabs my readers' attention.			
2. I state my opinion at the beginning of my paper.			
3. I include reasons for my opinion based on my own thoughts about the topic.			
4. I group connected ideas together.			
5. I use evidence from the text to support my opinion.			
6. I use linking words, signal words, and phrases to link ideas.			
7. I include a concluding sentence or paragraph that makes my readers think.			
8. My opinion follows an organized structure.			
9. I choose words that make sense and make my opinion interesting.			
10. I do not change my opinion.			
11. I use different types of sentences.			
12. I use my voice to show people how much I care about my opinion.			

Quality Writing Checklist

I looked for and corrected . . .	Yes	No	Not Sure
sentence fragments and run-ons.			
parts of speech (pronouns, auxiliaries, adjectives, prepositions).			
grammar.			
indented paragraphs.			
punctuation.			
capitalization.			
spelling.			

Notes:

Notes: